SEEING RED

SEEING RED

The autobiography of the actress

Coral Atkins

and her battles with and on behalf of
disturbed children

ANDRE DEUTSCH

First published in May 1990 by
André Deutsch Limited
105-106 Great Russell Street
London WC1B 3LJ
Second impression June 1990

British Library Cataloguing in Publication Data

Atkins, Coral
  Seeing red.
  1. England. Welfare work with children
  — Biographies
  1. Title
  362.7'092'4
  ISBN 0 233 98508 5

Printed in Great Britain by
Billing & Sons, Worcester

For Harry Whitehead

ACKNOWLEDGEMENTS

In my experience there is no such person as a disturbed child, there are only disturbing environments which force the child to adapt its otherwise normal behaviour to cope with them. I have never come across a bad child, or one whom it was impossible to love, and underneath all the pain and the rage I have never found a child who didn't possess a kind and generous heart.

In telling my story I have disguised my children as best I can to protect their privacy. I would like to sing their praises to the heavens, each and every one of them who have been, and still are, in my care. They have all seen the face of hell and survived. But their stories are for them to tell; enough for me to plead in my book for endless allowances to be made, and for second chances to be given to children who, through no fault of their own, find themselves abandoned to the wilderness of 'In Care', and then often blamed for being there.

If I have missed out any of the many friends who have helped me along the way, forgive me. Here I list just a few: Maggie Dawson, Pauline Munro, Patrick Carter, S. Stefan, Glenda Jackson, Sir Godfrey Nicholson, Martyn Read, Dorothy Wright, Pinkie Kavanagh, Barbara Flynn, Helen Kennedy, Vera Hankin, Rosie and the late George Smith, Connie Booth, Lady Meg Thomas and Mrs Haines of Twekesbury; Miss Langrish for the car; Directors, past and present; the Gyde Trust; the Variety Club; Marilyn, Barbara, Susie, Marion, Alan, Steve and Andy for their long-term care of the children; my sister, Sylvia, and her children, Kate and David; Harry's grandma, Zenia White-head, Alexander Schneider, who made me happy; my late father, Eric, who made me laugh and taught me a healthy disregard for the book of rules; and my mother, Lillian Louisa, who gave me so much love I had a little to spare one hot summer's day.

My special thanks go to Christopher Wayne Barrow — my hero — whose love, loyalty and sheer brilliance in working with the children can never be exaggerated, or the debt I owe him repaid.

Unutterable and nameless is that which torments and delights my soul and is also the hunger of my belly. I do not want it as a law of God, I do not want it as a human statute: let it be no signpost to super earths or paradises. It is an earthly virtue that I love: there is little prudence in it and least of all common wisdom.

But this bird has built its nest under my roof: therefore I love and cherish it, now it sits there upon its golden eggs.

Friedrich Nietzsche
Thus Spake Zarathustra

SEEING RED

Once upon a time there was a little girl with brown eyes and golden hair who lived with her mummy, daddy and sister in a place called London and whose daddy loved to paint pictures. One day he was painting her sister in a red cloak and, upon been asked what it was called, he took down a big fairy-story book from the shelf and showed her a picture of a girl rather like herself, in the same red cloak, setting off to visit her grandmother whose cottage lay in the middle of a large forest. How dark the forest seemed, and how glad she was that it was not she who had to make such a perilous journey alone as she snuggled deeper into the safety of her father's arms. The day had been a strange one, her parents busy and worried, and her mother packing her and her sister's clothes into a big brown case. What did it all mean? she wondered, but knew no fear, and, as her sleepy eyelids began to close, the last thing she saw with her mind's eye was the girl in the bright red cloak. Little did she know it then, but it would be many years and many adventures later before she would be able to see the colour red again.

ONE

On that June day in 1970 I was a star. A glorious, glistening, shining, never-fading star, who felt that on this newborn summer's morning she could, like the giraffe on a clear day, see for ever.

A star: showered with flowers, brass bands playing when I stepped off planes, fan mail by the bucketful. I was pursued endlessly through the streets by desperate shoppers who would clutch me to their tearful bosoms, wailing, 'You're me 'ole life, Sheila.' And ambitious mothers would push their small reluctant children towards me, ordering, 'Go on, tell 'er, tell 'er. Tell 'er what you was goin' to tell 'er. Tell 'er what I told you to tell 'er.' And the small reluctant ones would shuffle shyly forwards, mumbling, 'I've not missed an episode, Sheila.' ''E's not missed an episode, Sheila.' Not missed an episode (praise de Lord). I would smile and murmur sweet words of wonder and gratitude to all this and listen enthralled while they told me what they would like to do with my erring TV husband if they could lay their hands on him (chance would be a fine thing!).

'Leave 'im love. He's not worth it. I can see mental anguish writ all over 'er face. Can't you, Joyce?'

'Oh yes, she's suffered, love.'

''Ow you've suffered. You're sufferin' now aren't you, love? You are lovey. He's not worth it,' etc., etc., and so forth and so fifth, as my father would say.

Fame sat well on my shoulders. It fitted like a glove. It seemed

1

somehow normal to me. Recognition at last, and not before time. I was thirty-two on that June day and the heroine of a TV soap opera set in the Forties called A Family At War. I was 'Our Sheila'; downtrodden and betrayed, but lovely with it.

'She's lovely with it, ain't she Joyce?'

The story revolved around a family going through the war in Liverpool; mum, dad, three sons and two daughters. I played a daughter-in-law, married to the eldest son, a fighter pilot who felt himself to be a cut above the little woman at home and deceived her endlessly with his upper-class hussies. Oh, the agony. Oh, the tears. I'm particularly good at suffering bravely. Seldom a hair or a false eyelash out of place during the worst of the TV air-raids, the most violent family rows, or the wildest scenes of sex and lust. Yes, I had my priorities well in hand.

Things weren't always so easy for me, I must admit. Recognition came late and was hard won, my beginnings in the business being ''ard an' 'umble'.

At seventeen, I was a very reluctant art student at Winchester College of Art, hoping to emulate my father, Eric, six times exhibitor at the Royal Academy. But after two long years, with my National Diploma in Design exams approaching, I was having to admit to myself that whatever it took to make a painter, I didn't have it. Escape was the answer. Far, far away from the life class, the clay models and the dreadful and dreaded textile design lessons. The further the better.

'An actor's life for me'; a dream I had always nursed secretly to myself, since being chosen to play Shylock in the sixth-form version of The Merchant of Venice. (Shylock? Hang on a minute, why Shylock?) 'The pound of flesh, my life', stayed with me and when it led to my being chosen to narrate a luxurious production of The Creation and Noah at the town hall in Reading, my cup of theatrical joy was running over.

Fate was kind to this little would-be actress. My parents ran a newsagent's during this time. By chance, a copy of The Stage was delivered to our shop by mistake. No actors or actresses in our neighbourhood, but it was surely pounced on by me, and there, hallelujah, was an advertisement for a student actress, with Earl Armstrong's Strolling Players – no experience needed, but keenness and enthusiasm essential. Oh, I had them by the bucketful, and after some hassle with my parents – too young, too far away from home, what about my exams? etc., etc., – I took off for my first engagement in Tinygongal, North Wales. Scared, certainly. Shiver shiver and shake shake. Clutching my toy rabbit (well, I know, but I was only seventeen), I somehow got myself onto the train and away.

Earl Armstrong was a dear kindly man in his late sixties, with a seen-it-all, world-weary manner and a lazy, hang-dog, well-lived-in face, who was put out by very little, especially such unimportant things as forgetting his lines. He simply made them up as he went along, or borrowed lines from other plays until he got himself more or less back into the right one.

His wife was a different kettle of fish altogether. Small, four foot ten perhaps, seventy years old, with dyed hair. 'Hennaed, my dear. Not dyed, hennaed, hennaed.' Long curly eyelashes, nails like the Wicked Witch of the West and a temper to match, but she was a lady: a twenty-four carat, one hundred per cent genuine theatrical lady. Beautiful – well, as a butterfly – and as proud as a queen, she sailed through each play with such a ferocious dignity that only the most stout-hearted amongst us also-rans would dare to snigger as she took every lead, no matter what; and I found myself, in my first professional role, playing her nanny.

Mrs A.: Oh, Nanny, Nanny, may I go to the ball? After all, I am sixteen.

Me: Well now, I'm only an ol' woman an' I've lead a very narrow life.

Earl, of course, took all the male leads. We had one day to learn our lines, one rehearsal, then bingo, the big time, up and away, with the audience watching, in what I can only believe in retrospect to have been stunned silence. Anyway, they came, sat, watched and left without a sound. I loved it all, which was just as well because I had to do it all, practically: collecting the props, cleaning the stage and furniture – she liked her brasses shining – taking the money at the door, pulling the curtains, putting on the music and prompting. In between, of course, whizzing on and off stage as somebody's something. It was here I fell in love with a young leading actor who would hold my hand and walk on the mountains with me until a new male assistant stage manager joined the company. Then they held hands and walked on the mountains and I was very hurt and puzzled until an old experienced 'character lady' of nineteen took me to one side and told me the alternative facts of life, which left me for several days shocked into disbelief.

It wasn't too long before I too became an old cynic who felt herself to be far too good for all this rubbish and got fixed up in weekly rep. 'What do you do with the rest of the week, after you've learnt the play and rehearsed it?' was my first question.

I was taken on by Jack Bradley and his 'Uncle' Morris. Jack was in his late thirties, big, muscley, tatooed, toupéd; his uncle old, frail and given to taking a drop of Dutch courage now and again. Well, pretty well all the time, which led to many a bitter, hissing quarrel between the two of them. Like the Armstrongs, they owned the company and played more or less what they wanted, without regard to how suitable they may or may not have been for the parts. This resulted one week in Jack playing a sensititive fourteen-year-old prodigy violinist, clutching a Stradivarius in his massive, muscley, heavily tattooed arms (lions rampant, eagles in flight, Mother, Love, etc.). He liked a laugh, turning every play into a comedy, and could often be heard off-stage chuckling to himself as he planned some new gag to suprise us with on stage.

In *Mother of Men*, a savage drama about lust and incest, he would deliberately spill the tea, mop it up with a pair of knickers placed strategically on a guard-rail by the fire, then squeeze the knickers back into the pot and pour a cup of tea. His relationship with his uncle was strained and bitter. I recall one time when Morris, a little worse from a drop of the hard stuff, was on stage playing a murderer. Discovering that the

4

murder weapon had not been set where it should be, he wandered round the stage, wailing, 'The knife, the knife. I can't find the knife,' to which Jack hissed in a loud and furious stage whisper, 'Strangle her, you bloody fool!'

I didn't care. I had been promoted to juvenile lead and all the lovely, lovely parts came my way. My hair was long and golden, my skin tanned by the summer sun. People were beginning to leave notes for me at the stage door, and at least two men in the company were giving me the eye. One was a rather plump electrician whom I would force to skip, so that I could see his cheeks wobble. 'Skip, Joe. Skip.' And skip he did. The other was a fervent Scottish Nationalist, whom I would force to deny Scotland three times before I would let him take me out. Then I would laugh at the two of them, saying I would never go out with anyone so feeble. I was looking for a glorious, golden Rupert Brooke, the young Apollo of my early teens: a poet; a painter; a god. And I would save my precious little self for him.

Oh how lovely it was to be me! Going on eighteen and unstoppable, stronger and more confident with each new play. I stayed with Jack and Morris for almost a year, and on leaving and proudly producing my fully stamped-up insurance card for the Labour Exchange, discovered it certainly was fully stamped-up: with Brooke Bond tea stamps.

There was another actor in the company called J.J. who would also slavishly follow me around. I didn't like him much. I tried to avoid him, with his dark curly hair, grey eyes and yes, let's face it, large nose. He was persistent and intense, falling to his knees in Tonbridge High Street, climbing a tree outside my bedroom window to read me bits from *Tess of the Durbervilles*. Ah, powerful stuff. I tried hard to resist it, and although he hit me hard around the face on our first date, out of jealous fervour ('Oh Sheila love, you're a fool to yourself'), I married him.

Like a little rosebud that almost makes it to a rose, then seems to shut up shop and die, so, slowly, did I.

Oh grandmother, grandmother, what grey eyes you have.

All the better to see you, my dear.

J.J. was an angry man. He hated most things bitterly and loved a few with a giddy passion which he expected me to share. We continued to move around the country working in reps as a duet, like Anne Ziegler and Webster Booth, but without the harmony and out of tune. His temper usually got the better of him, and often got us the sack, building up more and more people to hate and more grudges to bear. At first I was one of the things included in the giddy passion, but in no time at all I was seen as far from perfect.

'Oh I will try harder, J.J., I promise. I really will try not to annoy you.'

Down and down I went, round and round I went, beginning to learn what shiver shiver really meant as I heard his key in the door. Was the house clean? Was the dinner what he wanted? Oh, had I forgotten something that he had told me to do? To fail on any of these counts could result in a thump or a kick or a slammed door and him gone for two days. I should have put the flags out when it was the latter, but I wept and cried and I loved him and I felt if only I could be a better person, he wouldn't be so troubled. His father was worse. The first time I met him, he was crouched by his fourth-floor-flat window with a pair of binoculars and a shotgun, and his first words to me, in thick Scouse, were, 'I'll bloody swing for 'er.' His wife apparently was sitting below in a car with a man from the Coal Board. Then he told me in confidence, 'Do you know, I married the three worst bloody women in the world.'

I took to going to church to get some advice from the good Lord on how best to cope with my predicament. 'Dear Lord, tell me how I should be. Tell me what I should do.'

'Take a baseball bat and smack him round the ear,' I thought I heard the still, small voice reply.

'Oh, surely not. What about Gentle Jesus forgive them that trespass against us, and black our eyes.'

'Now look what you've made me do.'

'Sorry J.J. Sorry I made you black my eye. Oh, forgive me, it's just that, well, you've got no sense of humour.'

'What do you mean I've got no sense of humour? I have got a sense of humour. I have got a sense of humour. I have, I have.' As I was snatched by the throat and shaken like a rag-doll.

Well, the harder I tried to please him, the more I got up his size-twelve nose. It seemed I could do nothing right, and the little bit of confidence I had from my profession was beginning to desert me so that I feared leaving the house. Any interviews I had loomed so large that I was a trembling jelly by the time I got to them. And if I didn't do it to myself, J.J. had ways of doing it for me. He would wait until I was all done up in my best dress, hair and make-up the very prettiest I could manage, then, as I kissed him, said goodbye and stepped outside the front door, he would just murmur, 'Oh!'

'What J.J.?'

'Oh! It's nothing really.'

'What's nothing?'

'It doesn't matter.'

I always fell for it. 'It does. It does matter. Oh what is it? Please, J.J., tell me. What is it?'

'Well, you're not going to an interview looking like that are you?'

You get my drift?

No, he wasn't all bad, and would on occasions be capable of great tenderness, bringing me a bunch of flowers now and again after he had been particularly unreasonable. But my humble gratitude would usually set him off again. Oh yes, there are always two sides to every story. His one great virtue was his loyalty to his friends. He would never let them down. Never, never, ever, whatever!

'He has a lot of integrity,' I once said in his defence. 'Yes,' replied my friend Pat, 'he's a seething mass of it.'

After five years or so, he decided to leave me. Who could blame him? I, of course, was heartbroken; weeping and sobbing and shaking until I thought I would almost lose my mind, living only for the phone to ring, the sound of the key in the door, and dropping two stone in weight – the only good thing that ever came out of a broken heart. For a year I lived like this, with him occasionally coming back, sweeping me up in his arms, saying he loved me, everything was going to be all right, he was coming home, etc. He would stay for a couple of days, then disappear for another three months, until, on one of his sweeping reunions, I heard a voice – could it have been that still, small one? – saying, 'I never want to see you again.' And I found myself running down the road, throwing myself through my friend Pauline's door and collapsing. She was very kind: put me to bed and kept me there for many many weeks until I was strong enough to face life again.

No, I don't blame J.J. He fell in love with a fiery, dignified eighteen-year-old, and ended up married to a twenty-five-year-old doormat.

Although kind, Pauline was firm with me. No way was I going back to my flat in Camden Town, where J.J. could come and go as he pleased. I was to stay with her until some alternative could be found. Too ill and fragile to argue, I lay in her big safe bed and allowed myself, for the first time in nine years, to be taken care of. An actress herself, and very busy, she still found time to make my well-being her priority and it was due in no small part to this that I was soon able to carry on with what was left of my career.

Ah, but life is not kind. It's not nice. It doesn't play by the Marquess of Queensberry rules. There are no rewards for virtue and kindness, no happy endings. As I grew stronger, and parts on television, etc., once again began to come my way, men gave me the eye again, which I now found amazing – 'Someone actually finds me attractive. Me. Somebody wants me for their play.' – so good a demolition job had J.J. done on my self-esteem.

Pauline arranged for me to share a flat for a while, with her latest paramour. 'You'll love him, Corrie. He's so beautiful. He's the most beautiful man I have ever seen, and I'm madly in love with him. It will be so good to have you sharing his flat.

8

You can keep an eye on him for me. He's called Peter Whitehead.'

Oh grandmother, grandmother, what blue eyes you have.

The first time I saw Peter, he was sitting on the floor in Pauline's flat, eating spaghetti. As I came into the room holding a glass of red wine, he looked up, tossed his thick blond hair from his face, and his heavy-lidded pale blue eyes locked into mine. I shook. I literally physically shook, so that the wine spilt down my new denim shirt.

'Miss Atkins,' he said, 'we meet at last,' and smiled such a smile that I wanted to rush out of the room, climb onto the roof, wave my knickers in the air and scream, 'Hallelujah! Bingo! Yeah hoo! Found at last – my golden and glorious dream of delight.' In fact, I mumbled something about having to change my shirt, got Pauline in the kitchen and said, 'No. Absolutely not.' No way was I going to share a flat with him. It just wouldn't work out. We would have to think of something else. I couldn't. I simply couldn't. I just didn't like him. I felt somehow, and I went on and on, (but not on and on and on and on and on!). She was adamant, and he simply smiled his devastating smile and said, 'You've got nothing to lose.'

'Except my life. Except my life.' And I finally agreed, reassuring myself that I was so plain, thin and boring at least he wouldn't fancy me, so perhaps if I tried not to look at *him*, maybe wore thick pebble glasses whenever he was around so that I couldn't see him properly, or eye-patches or something, well perhaps we could manage to live together without hurting Pauline.

Oh, but he was like the morning sun over Africa, as deep and mysterious to me as a Brazilian rainforest, and, in truth, I knew, as deadly as a coiled rattlesnake to this little country mouse. Well I packed my bags and moved into his shark-infested waters in Soho, where he lived in a tower (where else), and worked as a documentary film-maker.

My first memory of moving in is of the Baccanias Brazillieras

Number Five, playing loudly. A sad, pale girl sat on his big bed weeping; another emerged from the bathroom wearing knickers with a towel on her head, and yet another girl appeared at the door and was let in by the beknickered one.

'Eeh, chuck, get out of here while you can, Sheila love'.

No. I stayed. I made my small room there as comfortable as I could, with all the things I liked and no trace of J.J. or my wedding gifts. Well, I did by mistake take a box that J.J. had made to hold records. Jumped up and down on it a hundred times to break it up. It simply smirked up at me; with all that integrity in every screw, you must be joking!

I found the more I looked at Peter, the less I saw him. And when I discovered his favourite food was egg and chips, I knew that I had found a soul-mate. In truth, it was a great relief to Peter not to have to seduce me, and if ever a man needed a friend in those days it was him.

So much activity between the sheets – so little real concern out of them. I found him to be a passionate, clever man, full of joyful curiosity about every aspect of life, and the courage to risk all in pursuit of it. We became good friends and confidants, living in happy and harmonious platonicus for many many months. Both of us were beginning to do well, he with his documentary films, me now in a West End play. Life was so good, what could possibly spoil it?

We both had affairs – nothing important – and would sit up long into the night laughing and talking about our latest conquests and how little chance they had with us, my old confidence creeping slowly back to match his. We felt enchanted and all would have continued like this had it not transpired that I met Maximilian Schell, who thought so highly of me as an actress that he began trying to get me out of the play I was in at Wyndham's and into his at the Royal Court. Peter and I laughed about this, until I stayed out all night with Max. (Oh, very boring. He showed me endless photographs of himself and by six in the morning I had seen enough of them.) On reaching home with so much to tell Pete and make him laugh, I was

10

greeted by him in a state of furious, jealous rage: 'How could you stay out all night with Maximilian Schell? How could you do this to me?' and he smacked me round the head. (Too much high-quality competition.) I smacked him back instinctively. No one was ever going to hit me again.

Well of course the end of the story was that we landed up in each other's arms like any pair of decent lovers from a Mills and Boon novelette, wondering why it had taken us so long to see the obvious. So now I slept in the big round bed in the tower, like the Princess and the Pea, with my handsome Prince reading me Yeats and Rilke; telling me tales of the ancient Greeks and Romans, of Akhenaton and his sun god. He taught me to comprehend Einstein's theories. Yes, I actually grasped the old relativity junket, and, for my part, I brought him into the twentieth century a little.

He had never even heard of the Beatles when we met in 1965, but being a smart cookie and a brilliant film-maker was soon in great demand, making five-minute films of all the stars of the day for Top of the Pops and the like. I also taught him to laugh at himself a little and not to be quite so serious and intellectual, and I knew from the moment our eyes met that here was the father of my child, no one else would ever do.

After trying hard for a year, 'Oh the effort, oh what a drag,' I finally became pregnant and on 7 May 1967 the earth stopped turning, gave a hop, skip and a jump for joy and our son Harry Dominic Whitehead came into the world with a half-smile, a yawn, and I'm sure a wink at his mother. Nothing has ever topped that, or ever will.

'True love at long last, our Sheila.'

Well, not quite. We tried hard. We really tried hard, but as I became more and more pregnant and dependent, Peter became more and more successful. The flat was always full of the beautiful people. We were where it was 'at' in the Sixties, all of them coming to worship at his feet, captivated by his extraordinary magnetism.

Marianne Faithful wept there, Allen Ginsberg wrote a poem

11

there, Jimi Hendrix, the Beach Boys and Pink Floyd passed through on their way to fame, and I was relegated to tea lady. Not a very nice one, I confess. I recall with shame a day when, having made about one hundred pots of hash tea for the Rolling Stones, tripping backwards and forwards thinking how lucky I was to serve them – wow! the Stones! – I was suddenly overcome with a terrible feeling of resentment, opened the editing-room door where they were all making whoopee, and threw the hundred and first pot at them. It hit the light bulb, which exploded. They, thinking I had shot at them, dived under the editing table, then crawled out of the flat on their hands and knees, making signs of peace and love at me, and murmuring, 'Heavy scene, Peter man, like heavy scene.'

Luckily by now Peter had acquired a sense of humour. He laughed, and made me egg and chips, as I was on the whole a good-natured creature. I even invited one of his ex-wives to come and live with us, having met her, liked her and discovered she had nowhere else to go. All well and good. However, one morning I found a pile of suitcases in our hallway, accompanied by a young and very beautiful blonde Swedish girl. On inquiring who she was and being told she was yet another long-lost wife come to stay, I fear I chased both wives out with a steam-iron I was using on his shirts, then threw cases, ironing-board, shirts and iron after them.

'Phew,' replied Peter on hearing of all this, 'I've been trying to get rid of them for years!'

What a rat. Still, not all our quarrels ended so happily. It seemed that I now feared and resented the very parts of him I had at first loved and admired: his freedom, his courage and his honesty. I could no longer bear the truth; it hurt. Yet I began to check up on him, forcing him to lie to me. Oh, it's an old story. After nearly two years of living like this I began to wonder what kind of mother I was for this darling little golden-haired Harry I had been given. Always distracted, always suspicious or weeping, which of course drove Peter further away. I gave it a lot of thought, but knew finally that if I was ever going to make anything of my life, I would have to do it alone.

Peter did not have the strength to leave us, I knew. I would have to take the responsibility. So one day, after one of his long filming trips abroad, accompanied, as usual, by one of his Botticelli angels, I changed the locks on the flat, so he couldn't get in. It nearly killed us both. We sat on opposite sides of the door, weeping.

'What will become of you, without me?' we both generously wept, but I kept the door locked and curled up into a ball and waited for the pain to stop. I won't dwell on it, that gnawing pain that waits like toothache when you wake, dogs you through the day and is the last thing that you feel before sleep.

Oh grandmother, grandmother what sharp teeth you have. Please please, me, but not Harry. Please not my sweet Harry.

So now there were just the two of us. But an actress's life is seldom predictable.

One day down the Labour, skint:

'Name?'

'Coral Atkins.'

'Son's name?'

'Harry.'

'Father's name?'

Pause . . . if I say Peter Whitehead, they'll say go and find him, he's rich and famous, let him keep you. I didn't know where he was.

'Um, Whychauski.' What an inspiration!

'Um, Mrs Atkins, how do you spell that?' Blank stare . . .

'Well, we can't give you any money. The father must be found. Where is he?' Pause . . .

'Um, seeking for the meaning of life . . . In Tibet.' Long, long pause . . .

'So, er, what was his last known address?'

'Um, c/o the Dalai Lama?'

'Don't try to be funny with us, Mrs Atkins. Next please.'

'All right, all right. I'll take my poor, pale, sad son,' Harry leaping and gurgling with joy, shining like a little sunbeam; I give him a pinch, but it doesn't work, 'and I shall go and pick up men around the tube stations. How else can I feed him?' Murmurs of shame from everybody in the Labour Exchange.

'Mrs Atkins, come back, come back,' and £12.08 is pressed into my hand. Loud cheers from my fellow grafters.

Next day the script was dropped through my door. 'We would like you to read for the part of Sheila, in . . .' Oh and I'd got it and before you could hardly spend £12.08 I was a star.

Yes, a star, as I strolled round a fête on a June day in 1970. The day that Chicken Licken was proved right. The sky did fall in. On me.

TWO

The actress tossed her mane of long blonde hair back from her face, smiled her by now familiar, winning smile, and heard herself saying, 'Really? And how many children do you have here in the Home?' as she glanced surreptitiously at her watch, and wondered how soon she could slip away.

The day was hot for early June and it was almost an hour since she had declared the fête open, made her polite little speech, signed over a hundred autographs and ooh'd and ah'd at all the stalls. The flowers she had been presented with were by now beginning to wilt. Five more minutes, she thought. Five more minutes, and I'm off. So many more important things were on her mind – the script for the next episode which she hadn't even opened yet, her part had better be bigger this week than last or she'd have to complain. After all, it was she who got all the fan mail, she was the one the public obviously wanted to see. Then there was the trip to Sweden to sort out and the offer of a film there for her in the autumn. Must find out more about that. Oh, and Steve, he was really beginning to scare her. He seemed to be taking their affair so seriously. She would have to watch out, maybe move flat. Didn't want her son to have to listen to any fights between her and her lovers. Peace and quiet. Must phone her agent. She really should change her agent.

'Most of the children come here from broken homes, of course, Miss Atkins, and live full-time, unless we can find suitable foster parents.'

'I see, yes,' said the actress. 'Well, they all seem happy enough.' She watched the children as they ran excitedly around the gardens.

'Oh yes. Lots of staff here to take care of them.' The man by her side droned on. The steel band banged their dustbin lids, and the sun seemed hotter than ever. To get away from all this, she excused herself and wandered into the large old Victorian house; once a vicarage, now a home for problem children.

Peering into one or two of the grey, bare rooms, she soon felt she had seen enough and was about to leave when she thought she heard the sound of sobbing from one of the rooms at the end of a long corridor. As the sound increased, she found herself running towards the room, wondering what terrible tragedy she would find on the other side of the door.

The room was large and bare, except for several plastic tables and chairs lined along each wall, and, at the far end, a kitchen of sorts, with cooker, cupboards and a worktop, upon which sat two pleasant-looking women, chatting amiably and sipping tea, while under one of the plastic tables crouched a little girl of maybe five or six, sobbing and screaming and throwing herself from side to side in a frenzy of panic, pressing closer and closer to the wall as if she would like it to open up and swallow her to safety. The actress stood for a moment on the threshold, unable at first to grasp that this was real, and not a part of some scriptwriter's nightmare; surely some phantom director would soon call 'cut', and everybody would laugh and congratulate the little girl on her performance. Calling to the two women to help her, she flung herself down by the child. The two ladies sprang instantly to life.

'Oh, I say Joyce, it's Sheila! Oh, what an honour. Miss Atkins, I was only saying to Joyce here, I hope we get a glimpse of 'er. Wasn't I, Joyce?'

'Yes, she was.'

'Oh, I love your series. When your husband left you for that London woman, I cried buckets. Didn't I?'

'Yes she did. She's so soft. An ol' softy that's what I call 'er, Sheila. An ol' softy.'

'What's wrong with her?' screamed the actress again and again as she tried to take the little girl in her arms; blind now to all but her terror. 'What have you done to her?'

One of the women came over and said in a quiet, confidential manner, 'I wouldn't bother with 'er, lovey, if I was you. You'll get your nice dress all dirty. She does that now and again. Best to leave 'er. She'll be all right in half an hour or so.'

'But she's terrified. Can't you see? She's terrified.' The child by now was clawing at the walls; her little fingers all cut and bleeding.

'Well, you see Sheila – may I call you Sheila? – she brings it on herself. Wants to make coffee all the time. Says she has to. Well we restrain her, of course. So she goes under there and she screams.'

'Why? Why does she want to make coffee?'

The women stared blankly at each other before one replied, 'Who knows with these little kiddies. You never know.'

'But who takes care of her?' demanded the actress, tears now streaming down her face as she tried to catch the child's hands.

'Well there's six of us on nine 'til four, then night staff come on duty. So you see there's plenty of people to look after her. There's no need to get yourself all upset.'

By now the actress had managed to get her arms around the child and rock her backwards and forwards, kissing her little bleeding fingers and murmuring, 'Hush-a-bye, hush-a-bye. You shall have all the pretty little horses. All the pretty little horses.' – her own son's favourite lullabye. The screams began to subside, and little by little the actress felt the child allowing herself to be comforted, sobbing and sighing still, but beginning to lean a little more heavily into her arms. They continued to sit there, the child and the actress, under the plastic table, clinging to each other as if the world itself would come to an end if they let go.

The big guns were called! The matron strode in: big, bustly

17

and full of good northern common sense. 'I do appreciate, of course, Miss Atkins, you taking a personal interest in the children, but they're much better off left to the experts. Joyce, take her. C'mon. Take her. We're not having all this fuss.'

And they led the child away – silent and broken, her little body still racked by soundless sobbing – neither roughly nor kindly, but with indifference, as they continued their animated conversation on 'Our Sheila'. How they couldn't get over having her here in the room with them, and what they'd like to do with her erring television husband if they could lay their hands on him.

The matron continued her down-to-earth banter. 'They have to learn to live in the real world, these children. All this making coffee. We have rules. She knows the rules. Of course, you can't expect too much after the family she comes from. Father a hopeless alcoholic, always beating her and her mother up, 'till we took her into care. Probably has some brain damage. Her behaviour just doesn't make sense, but she has to live in the real world, Sheila. By the way, Miss Atkins, or can I call you Sheila? I hope I may ask you this, but could I have your autograph? It's not for me you understand, it's for my mother. She loves your series. She hasn't missed an episode. And you, well, may I say, you're her whole life, Sheila.'

The actress, too, is silent and broken, and as she leaves the room she looks round and sees all that is left of her vanity – a bouquet of wilted flowers and a large straw hat abandoned on the kitchen floor.

She put up a good fight, the actress in me. 'Go back. Get your flowers and your hat and get on with your life. You're winning,' she whispered. 'You have a series to finish, rehearsals tomorrow, a script to read and no time for weeping over lost causes. You must pull yourself together.'

But I couldn't hear her. All I could hear were the screams of the child. All I could see, the cold indifferent faces of my public. Were these, then, the people who fanned the flames of my vanity? Was it for them I primped and preened in front of the mirror; that I rehearsed my part, hour after endless hour, to get it just right, so that these people could escape from their 'fantasy' world of caring for little frightened children, into a 'real' one, where Sheila and her husband fought it out and true love conquered all?

I recalled a line of Friedrich Nietzsche's – something about the thing that gives you greatest happiness needing to justify existence itself – and understood for the first time the enormity of what it meant. He knew about love. Not the namby-pamby, gentle Jesus kind, but the kind that has the courage to stand up and be counted: to live outside the confines of praise or blame. All the qualities I lacked. No Mighty Warrior, me; no queen of lost causes. Be nice to everybody, and everybody will be nice to you, that was my motto. Always smile at rehearsals. Always agree with the directors. A joy to work with. The odd tantrum now and again, for the sake of appearances, but that was all.

I tried hard to put the child out of my mind, but found myself telephoning the Home again and again, to see what I could do. I even called round there, but was met with a stone wall.

No, I couldn't see her. No, there was nothing she needed. And finally, in desperation, after asking if I could have her for a while because I knew why she screamed, I was told angrily by the matron that I was making the fundamental mistake that all untrained people make. 'I tell all my staff, right from the start, Miss Atkins: they must not get emotionally involved with these children. What these kind of children need most is the detached professional approach.'

'Let me have her,' I pleaded again.

'And what about all the others?' she said. 'I've got at least a dozen more like her. You can't take them all.'

Yet neither could I go on living in a world where this kind of misery was condoned as policy, and do nothing. I would be worse than the women. They couldn't see what they were doing, but I could. I knew why the little girl screamed and why she needed to make coffee, and I knew what would happen if she

19

didn't get the help she needed. It would end in madness. And if I professed to love my own darling son, Harry, what kind of love was it that extended only to him and could stretch its boundaries no further, encompass no one else? Surely all children were the same, needed the same total passionate love I gave him for as long as he wanted it. There were no such people as 'these kind' of children, who deserved at best 'detached indifference', at worst downright cruelty.

The actress threw in the towel in the end. Knowing that I had to trap myself somehow or I'd never go through with it I took a deep breath, picked up the telephone, called the Granada press office and declared to the world in general, or anyone who was interested, that I, 'Our Sheila' from Family at War, was opening a home for disturbed children. Ha, then I really did tremble. Get out of that one, Miss High and Mighty Actress, if you can!

The press loved it. I was hailed as a heroine from Stockholm to New South Wales. 'Actress Gives Up Silver for Gold.' 'Family at War Star, to Go to War for Kids,' etc. I hadn't actually done anything yet. My friends had all edged quietly away from me, thinking I'd gone mad, or got Religion and become a born-again Christian, while I set about searching for a house.

It must be big, preferably nearby so I could get all those children from that ghastly home, settle them in the new house and look after them properly. It never seemed a big deal to me once I'd made up my mind. Tuck them all up in bed safely and then get on with my life. Well there were no big houses in Manchester, or Withinshaw, or Chorlton-cum-Hardy, or even Walley Range. I had to search further afield, and who would believe it (not Sigmund Freud, certainly) but quite by chance I discovered just the house near my home town. A twenty-roomed thatched cottage, set in three acres of land, in the middle of nowhere. No, not for sale, I didn't have that kind of money. For rent, on a long lease to a suitably respectable tenant: me! Praise the Lord!

I never mentioned children when I met the landlords, just to be on the safe side. They were all rather grand so I said that I too was very grand and needed space for entertaining.

'Still, Miss Atkins. Twenty rooms and just you and your son. How will you fill them?'

'I'll think of something,' I murmured vaguely, and rushed back to rehearsals bursting to tell somebody about it. But who? Who? Who could I tell?

I told the other actors.

'Gosh! That's terrific, love. By the way, that line on page three when you say "Oh!", could you come in a bit quicker, only Christ I'm left with bloody egg on my face.'

So I told my current boyfriend, an actor in the series, who was now, alas, heavily into drink and tranquillizers for his nerves.

'It's fucking marvellous, love, fucking brilliant, and I'm going to fucking well help you.' I'd come two drinks too late. Pissed again.

'No Steve, really, I must go it alone.'

'One of these days,' he screamed at me, swallowing a fistful of tranquillizers, and washing them down with a quadruple whisky, 'you're gonna need my strength.'

Funniest man I'd ever met and the best actor in the show, when sober. When drunk, he made J.J. look like Andy Pandy. In one episode, when Our Sheila fought back and took a boyfriend, on being introduced off the set to the actor playing same, Steve simply blacked his eye. No messing around with rubbish like 'How do you do?' We had to write a line in the script about him walking into a lamp post in the blackout.

It wasn't so funny when he crow-barred his way into my flat one night, after a drunken orgy, and smashed my head against the wall again and again as he yelled in my ear: 'I love you. Don't you realise I love you?' I was rescued by a big black sheet-metal worker living next door, who rushed me off to hospital with a split head, my once-white dressing gown now blood red. Two hours later, Steve turned up at the same hospital, having gone home, taken an overdose of his tranquillizers, written in

21

blood (red felt-tip actually) all over his flat, 'Coral Atkins did this to me' then lain down in his doorway with the door open, all in black, like Hamlet (I love actors) and waited to die, or for his flatmate to get back from nightshift.

So there we lay, Mr and Mrs Smith, in different wards, knowing next day we had to film a scene where my character had to visit his in hospital after his plane has been shot down. We both arrived by ambulance, me with my hair all matted with blood, covered by a dreadful hat – the hat I simply couldn't forgive him for – and Steve weak and dazed from his 'orrible ordeal.

'Where am I? What day is it? Who are you?'

'You're in Granada studios, Steve. It's Monday, 11th July, and I'm Derek the director, and if you continue to suffer from amnesia, I shall be forced to cut your lines and ground your aeroplane.'

This was going too far. His scenes in the cockpit were his raison d'être.

'Jocks away boys. Angels one-five. We've got one shot at Gerry and one shot only. Then fly these old crates, like bloody hell, back to Blighty. Got that chaps?'

'Roger, Squadron Leader. Oh, and by the way, sir – good luck.'

Close up of Steve's face. Is that a tear in his eye? Close in on large picture of Our Sheila looking worried.

'Ah, Derek, love. Don't you think the last shot should be on my character's face, not Sheila's? Not that I care, of course,' etc., etc. Threatened with banishment from this lofty Eden, Steve soon remembered who he was and where he was and which side his powdered egg was margarined on!

It was all so much piffle to me compared to the new house, to which I rushed each weekend with Harry, two paintbrushes and lots of paint. We set about the twenty rooms – me painting the tops and Harry the bottoms. The house hadn't been lived in for five years and ivy had grown all over the windows, blocking out the light. There was no electricity, and at night, with only candles for comfort, Harry and I clung closely together with a hammer under the pillow for any real intruders and a prayer that any ghostly ones would stay away at least until the lights worked.

Harry was a real trooper. Only three and a half, but I already felt safe with him there. 'Pull yourself together, Coral,' he would say. 'It's only a little mouse or a bird,' every time I jumped at shadows. We sang songs about the Grand Old Duke of York and his ten thousand men to keep our spirits up. I wish they'd come marching in here and paint this damn blasted house instead of me, I thought desperately, never a one for hard work at the best of times. I cursed and swore as I painted and Harry sang, 'Hush-a-bye, don't you cry, and pull yourself together.'

Then the US cavalry arrived in the form of a crazy family called the McKinnons, who had read about me in a paper in Africa and had come over to help. Between us, and my sweet parents who helped when they could, although they too thought me quite mad, we went through the rest of the house like a dose of salts.

My father's colour schemes were a trifle suspect to say the least and had to be kept a close eye on. Being an artist, he had no interest whatsoever in his immediate surroundings, finding them of no importance. A packet of fags, a box of paints and a canvas, and Rimsky-Korsakov on the gramophone, and the world was his oyster. Sent to buy paint, he had been known to demand, 'Two tins of paint, miss,' and when asked what colour, to reply, 'Colour! Colour! Any bloody colour! Just wrap them up.'

So my rooms would end up lime green and petal pink. And strictly a one-coat man was Eric. Couldn't think what was wrong with one coat of lime green paint over twenty-five-year-old red and gold flock wallpaper.

'Bloody women!' he would say, lighting up another fag.

'Bloody women!' Harry would echo, and they would stroll goodnaturedly up the garden discussing loftier subjects.

'Did you know, Harry, that there are forty million nails made every second? Forty bloody million nails!'

'Jesus H. Christ, Grandy!' my little treasure would reply. And

23

they would lean together on the gate contemplating the enormity of it all, while my mother sang about Jesus wanting them both for a sunbeam.

'Not me!' yelled Harry. 'But,' he thought it over for a while, 'I might be a moonbeam.'

As the bombs continued to fall on the Ashton house on TV, so the new house began to take to shape. My mother cut the ivy from the windows and polished until the lattice panes shone. The McKinnons and I painted and papered everything in sight; pink and flowers for girls, blue and trains and cars for boys. Harry and Eric put up the odd picture and pulled out the odd weed, and we all went round junk shops buying furniture and painting it all to match everything and I began to feel really proud and happy. I had now been put into hiding firmly out of Steve's way, with a chauffeur and a bodyguard. Granada didn't want me getting into any more romantic battles until the series was over. In any case, they had sent Steve off to join Monty in the Western Desert, and when he had won that war he was sent back to his fancy woman in London. Imagine what a field day Our Sheila had, suffering over that, but it was nothing compared to the suffering that was going on in another part of the forest.

For some time now the actors playing Ma and Pa Ashton in the series – both dear people but like chalk and cheese – had not been hitting it off and it came to a head one day when the actress playing Mrs Ashton screamed, 'Get me out of this!' No, she didn't want to be written out but killed off. We warned her. We did warn her: 'Don't do it; don't die. Think of all those endless graveside scenes as the camera zooms in on dad's grief-stricken face. You'll be playing right into his hands.' We were right. He mourned her for the next ten episodes, suffering in heroic silence in the kitchen, in the bedroom, poking the fire, pouring out the tea. There was no end to the places he could mourn her in and just when we thought we had all seen the last of this tragedy, out came the old actor's integrity ploy – ah, we all do it – 'Umm, Derek me old son. I'm just a bit worried that Dad seems to be getting over Mother a bit too quickly. After all, she's only been gone a year.'

It seemed more like forty.

'Good point, Charles love. Good point. What we need is another scene showing him grieving for her. Nothing obvious, he's a very private man.'

'Oh, sure, sure. Very private grief.'

'Oh, absolutely.'

'But in large close-up.'

'What love? Oh, of course, yes. Naturally.'

Slow pan in on his tragic face as he's putting out the cat. Never in the history of human grief had so much been seen to be suffered by so few for so long and in such large close-up. She should have gone to her sister in Cleethorpes as the writer suggested. Dad couldn't have shed many tears over that.

The great day arrived. The house was finished. It beamed and it sparkled and it seemed to sing to me of happy times just around the corner and I thought about the next step. Someone had told me that I had to be something called registered, so I duly applied to the head office of the DHSS in London, who informed me curtly that, yes, that was so and that they would send someone down to inspect me the following week. We were all so excited. Pat and John and Martin and Jackie McKinnon rushing around doing little final odd jobs, my mother picking armfuls of wild flowers to put everywhere and Harry and Eric off somewhere watching the trains go by. They were both fed up with me, my house and my plans by now.

'Bloody kids,' they both yelled as they shot off down the drive in Eric's two-tone Ford Zephyr.

I awoke early on the morning of the inspection and as always my first thoughts on such an occasion were, 'What shall I wear?', not being quite sure how to appear. Sexy and glamorous; plain and ruddy-cheeked in sensible shoes; or casual in jeans and T-shirt – or would they think I hadn't tried if I did that? My only experience of being inspected was going for acting jobs, when you always dressed up to the nines, so that's what I opted for in the end. Be yourself, I thought, sticking on my false eyelashes and glancing happily out the window at the lovely summer sky. I froze. In the driveway was an old battered Rover which I recognised at once. Steve! How on earth had he found out where I lived? What idiot had given him my address and why today, God, of all days in the year, in the century? I rushed downstairs comforting myself with the thought that it was only 9.30. a.m. He couldn't be drunk, which was something, and maybe if I promised him anything, yes anything, if he went away for a couple of hours, it would still be okay. The scene in the kitchen banished any such comfort from my mind. Someone had given me a crate of champagne to celebrate my registration. Three of the bottles were rolling around empty on the floor; a fourth was missing. I soon found it and him flat out on the sitting-room carpet, dead to the world. Oh sweet Jesus, a drunken actor lying around the place was hardly going to impress anyone and God forbid if he should wake up, anything was possible, the least of which would be him following me around the house screaming 'Slag!' at the top of his voice. I couldn't put him in any of the rooms as they all had to be inspected. There wasn't anywhere else. There was. I suddenly remembered the cellar, which had a lock on the outside, and making a bed of sorts down there, I dragged and pleaded and cajoled him in.

'Fucking old slag,' he said fondly. 'I've come to help you fucking celebrate.'

'Great. Good. Have some more champagne. Have lots. Here, let's open another bottle.' And so I put him out once more, and not before time. I had just shut the cellar door and turned the key in the lock when I heard a car turning into my drive. Keep calm, I told myself, and remember they're on your side. It's just a formality.

The two ladies who emerged from the car didn't look in the least forbidding, both middle-fifties with neat suits and silk blouses and pleasant smiles on greeting me. It's going to be all right, I thought joyfully as I introduced myself and thanked them most profoundly for coming.

'So kind of you,' I said.

'No,' replied the older one. 'It's our job to check out all new ventures. So no, it has nothing to do with kindness.'

Well put in my place I began to show them round, chatting nervously about my plans for this room and that, and wobbling perilously all the while in my high-heeled shoes. The ladies checked and measured everything they saw. I thought for one wild moment they might run the tape measure over me! Nothing missed their trained and critical eyes and when we had once again returned to where we had started, avoiding the cellar, they looked at me sharply and smiled.

'Well, Miss Atkins,' said the spokeswoman pleasantly. 'It simply won't do, will it? And neither, my dear, to put it bluntly, will you.'

I continued smiling, unable at first to grasp what I had just heard. These weren't the words I had been expecting.

'I'm sorry,' I said. 'I don't quite understand.'

'I said it quite plainly. No! It won't do.'

'You mean the kitchen,' I continued anxiously, still not quite believing what my heart was beginning to tell me was actually happening as it missed a beat.

'The whole house. It's all wrong. I'll start with the bedrooms. All shapes and sizes. There are rules about sleeping children in care. So many square feet per child. Then take the inglenook fireplaces, freestanding beams, thatched roof, not to mention the location. All quite unsuitable for these kind of children.'

'And a grandfather clock!' chimed in the younger one incredulously.

'Then,' continued the older one, 'there's you. You have no qualifications. No experience. A young son to bring up alone, I believe.' I nodded miserably. 'And in the most unstable profession known to man. Taking care of severely disturbed children is a highly skilled job. It requires trained, qualified and thoroughly experienced people and there is simply no way we would entrust any of them to you.'

27

With that, she swept out, closely followed by the other one who turned and said kindly, 'And really, dear, there aren't enough loos.'

The car drove away. Nothing. No sound but the ticking of that grandfather clock, as I felt myself falling to my knees and heard from deep within me the sound of my sobs. On and on. Had I so many unshed tears inside me? I felt bereft and abandoned in a sea of panic, weeping for myself and the child and for all lost children. Weeping at my own ignorance and stupidity in believing that a world which could let my little girl's screams go unheeded under that table would be impressed by a silly vain actress with nothing to back her up but passion and naivety. What a fool I'd been. Was there ever a bigger fool than me?

This is where the story should have ended. I should have picked myself up and got on with my life as an actress. I would have liked to, and could have done so then with dignity, having at least tried. But I reckoned without that deep mysterious river which runs through us all, deeper than reason, passion or fear, binding us together and transcending every need but survival; the necessity for justice.

Justice, for the children, was to be loved. Where and by whom was immaterial. Justice for me was to be given the chance to love them. Nothing more or less would do. I have no other way of explaining my actions from then on. I was fuelled and fired like a rocket and nothing could stop me. Having first thrown Steve off my property I went confidently into the office, got out the telephone book and made a list of all the local dignitaries in a twenty-mile radius of the house. Somebody out there was going to help me. I picked up the telephone. It took three weeks and forty-seven telephone calls to Lord This, Lady That, Doctor and Mrs This and the other, before I dialled Sir Godfrey Nicholson MP's number. He picked up the telephone himself and after I had got halfway through my spiel, he said,

'Hold on a minute, I must see all this for myself. I'll be right over.'

A man in his late seventies, faithful spaniel by his side, every inch the English gentleman. I poured out my heart to him, explaining how the little girl had needed to make coffee because her mother, I was sure, did that to sober up her father. When the child was threatened or afraid it was her way of taking care of herself, and by stopping her and giving her no safe alternative they were driving her crazy. He heard me out, and then sat silently for a while. I held my breath.

'Well,' he said at last. 'It all makes good straightforward common sense to me, young lady, but there is somebody I want you to meet first and, if he agrees with me, I'll help you.'

I leapt up to hug him, not noticing his arm was in a sling.

'Little accident, parachuting over France,' he remarked casually. 'A hobby of mine.'

Oh how I loved him!

The man he sent me to see was Dr O'Gorman, head of two large psychiatric hospitals and a specialist in disturbed children. He too heard me out and seemed amazed by the things I said.

'You've been reading Winnicott, haven't you?' he laughed.

'What's that?' I said, thinking it must be a kind of *Who's Who*.

'Not what, who. He's a child analyst and his way of working with children is a lot like yours.'

He took a couple of books from the shelf. 'Read them. I think they may help you become a heavyweight. And yes, Coral, I would certainly send children to you. I believe they would be in safe hands.'

Next he looked over the house, advising me on the necessary alterations to bring it into line with accepted premises. No, the inglenook stayed, as did the free-standing beams and the thatched roof, but there were quite a few things which had to be done, and so I set about raising the money to do them.

I needed around £10,000 for all the work, which was a fortune in 1971. Although I was busy on another series by now, with Edward Woodward, I still wasn't earning that kind of money. Eddie being a nice man, and hearing of my predicament, offered to help by becoming my first chairman of the board and lending his name to my notepaper, and a dear actor called Geoffrey Chater gave me a cheque for £200, my first donation. However, some very serious fundraising still needed to be done.

About this time I was asked to receive an award for Family at War. Luckily for me, the ceremony at the annual TV awards was televised, so I used the occasion to appeal for help. Then I took up an invitation to visit Scandinavia where I did a whistle-stop tour of Denmark, Norway, Sweden and Finland, doing anything I could and charging heavily for it: opening supermarkets, promoting cars and factories, kissing old men and donkeys and anything else in sight, so long as it paid well. Then I came back to England and did the same there, selling myself up and down the country quite ruthlessly, until ten months later I had collected enough money to begin again.

More loos, eh? I put in four more. Asbestos under the thatched roof, fire-doors and sprinklers and fire-alarms everywhere. But I drew the line at turning the bedrooms into dormitories. Children come in all shapes and sizes and sleep in rooms of all shapes and sizes. I would have to argue that one out when the time came.

My new-found board of directors, Sir Godfrey Nicholson, Dr O'Gorman, Eddie Woodward and now Stefan, my greatest ally, a dear, crazy Pole I'd met through a friend of Dr O'Gorman, gave me all the encouragement they could and, thus armed, I called once again on the DHSS. First of all they refused to have anything at all to do with me, but after I had bombarded them with appeals they agreed reluctantly to look again at the house. No high-heeled shoes this time. No drunken actors hiding in cupboards. A heavyweight. I showed them round with confidence and though they sniffed a bit, they had to agree that at least the house was up to scratch. Now for me.

'Be at head office on Monday morning at 10.00. a.m., when

you will be examined by a board of our experts and, well, good luck.'

Human! They were human! But when Monday came I was a quivering mass of uncertainty again and when introduced to their board of experts shook in my sensible shoes.

A child psychiatrist, a clinical psychologist, a psychiatric social worker and three heads of department.

Oh Grandmother, Grandmother.

Still, at least I had read Winnicott.

The questioning began and they were relentless. The onus was on me to prove myself, not on them to make allowances. So be it. After three hours, the head shrink pushed back his chair, shook his head and laughed.

'I don't think there's any way we are going to stop you, Miss Atkins, is there? I believe we are going to have to say yes.'

Nods from all round the table. Smiles too and with one reservation they gave in, granting me my licence but insisting that I employ one qualified member of staff. Chickenfeed, whatever they wanted. I flew home in a cloud of euphoria, snatched up my most precious possession and kissed and hugged him, telling him that nothing mattered more than him, but his old mum had won.

'Get off,' he growled, 'and hand me my green silk spotted tie.'

So out we went to celebrate. Egg and chips, knickerbocker glories and coke floats all round. Then I set off to find the little girl who had first woken me from my slumbers and taught me that, though God may well be in his heaven, all was not well with the world.

THREE

It was June again, but it was 1972 by now, and though I searched diligently for more than a month I could find no trace of the little girl. The staff at the home had changed several times. I didn't even know the child's name. This was one defeat I had to face, but it was a bitter, bitter one. All I could do was pray that whoever's hands she had fallen into would be as kind and gentle with her as she needed and deserved. I returned home to the house, which in truth had been for her, and waited to see what would happen next. Not too long to wait. The telephone rang. It was a social worker asking, was she correct, did I take severely disturbed children?

Is the Pope Catholic? Yes, yes, yes, yes, yes, yes, yes! I wanted to scream. Don't put the phone down. Anything you need? Champagne, caviar? I'll be right over. Instead I replied gravely, 'You're quite correct. We do.'

She then described a little girl of three and a half she would like me to see. 'But I must warn you, Miss Atkins, no one else in the county will keep her. She has been everywhere.'

Nobody of three and a half can be that bad, I thought. We arranged a date to meet at the assessment centre where she was staying. A grim place by any standards; not a grandfather clock in sight, stone or wooden floors, steel-backed chairs in a semi-circle around an old television set, iron beds set in rows with one locker per child. Cold Comfort Farm.

'She screams all the time,' they told me.

'So would I if I had to live here,' I wanted to say.

'No one can control her.'

Expecting to see Lucretia Borgia, I was amazed and delighted to be introduced to a beautiful little girl with long dark hair playing in a corner of the room with Play-doh. Jody.

'Hello,' I said. She looked up at me from under her long fringe and laughed, squeezing the Play-doh a little harder.

'Who are you?' I said.

She made a snatch for my handbag, but was forestalled by one of the staff.

'It's all right,' I said. 'She can have it.'

Oh foolish me! It was ripped open and turned upside down before one of Eric's nails had been made, let alone forty million. She then put it on her head and ran shrieking with laughter into the garden, all of the staff in hot pursuit. Who could help admiring such spirit. I'll take her, I thought, without a second's hesitation. While I was waiting for my bag to be retrieved, I noticed another child of about five or so lurking behind a door and watching me closely. I called her over, asking her name, and discovered that she was Jody's sister, Ann.

'Nobody likes me,' she said sullenly, her head down. 'They only like her. She gets everything.' A tear began to run down her cheek. Oh, Lord, I hadn't thought of this happening, but there was only one solution.

'I want them both,' I said firmly.

'But it isn't policy. We can manage her sister. It's only Jody who needs specialised care.'

'Both or nothing.' I was adamant. They agreed. My first two children.

They were right. Jody did scream day and night, and when she wasn't screaming she laughed hysterically. Nothing else. No shades in between. Plunging perilously between terror and ecstasy, with nothing and no one to catch her. I discovered she had been left in the hospital at birth and before she was one year old had been moved twelve times, from hospital to hospital, nursery to nursery, then shunted between foster homes, children's homes, assessment centres and reception centres with no one single solid person in her short little life. People had no meaning for her, except as providers of the things she needed to divert her temporarily from the state of black lonely terror she lived in. The ecstasy over any new thing soon gave way to terror as its powers to divert her wore off. There was no way to comfort her. Human touch meant nothing, only a new thing would do. This ghastly vicious circle had to be broken. I could think of only one way this could be done. Each time she screamed for a new thing we had to say no, but instead give her a person, her own same person who would be there for her day and night for as long as it took. Her sister Ann simply followed in her slipstream, being less difficult to handle, getting less attention. She was a bubbling cauldron of resentment and quite rightly so. It wasn't fair. The telephone rang and rang.

An eight-year-old boy, Marcus, came next, with night terrors. No sooner did he fall asleep than his eyes opened and he would rush screaming through the house pursued by the very real demons of his dreams. I found him in a children's home where he told me he spent the night in the lavatories with toilet paper stuffed in his mouth to stop the screams, so fearful was he of the staff if he woke them.

We made a nightly ritual of going round the house together making sure all the doors and windows were locked so no real intruder could get in. Then we set about tackling the imaginary ones by building a tent for him in his bedroom to help him feel safe and enclosed, and one of us always slept in there with him until he felt safe enough to face the night alone.

So many children, so many tales of horror, and, to my mind, so many villains. Never before had I had a glimpse behind the net curtains of suburbia and what I saw shocked me to the core of my being.

Then, would I see a little girl of three? Her five previous foster placements had broken down over a twelve-month period. Reasons given, she showed no affection for her foster mothers. I went to see her in the neat little house with its yellow-painted door where she was then living. Amy, with her light blonde hair, glasses with one eye patched out, her little shoulders up and head down.

'She never even looks at me,' wailed the foster mother. 'I've tried everything for six whole weeks.' The child's arms were all bruises. I asked why. 'Yes, well, I admit I did hit her. She shows me no affection whatsoever.' Her own two children skipped into the room, hugs and kisses and biscuits.

'We've all tried, haven't we girls?' The girls nodded, snatched up the packet of biscuits and were gone.

'What a pair,' the woman laughed.

I looked at Amy. Why did she move me so? I felt my heart would break as she stood in front of me awaiting her fate in patient resignation and I wanted to spring at the woman's throat like a tiger. But you don't do that kind of thing in child care. Instead I smiled and said I would take her there and then, this very minute. Please fetch her things.

She said nothing to me on the journey home and, on reaching there, didn't move from the car until asked to do so. Then she stood shyly by the door at a loss to know what to do, still with her eyes fixed to the floor. I asked her if she would like to see her room, putting my arms round her. She stiffened and began to shake.

'I have to wash my hands next,' she whispered, so quietly I hardly heard her, and thus I witnessed for the first time the fearful washing ritual she was forced to go through every hour or so to keep herself safe, sometimes taking half an hour to wash one little hand. To stop her would result in her hiding in a corner with her hands over her face, shivering and howling like a trapped animal.

Who did this to you, Amy? Behind which of those nice neat painted doors did this happen to you? Who could I blame? Who kill? Don't get emotionally involved – what a joke. Try and stop me. We treated her with tenderness and care as she crept silently round the house on tiptoe, asking for nothing, saying nothing except to whisper from time to time, 'I'm a good girl. I'm a clean girl,' and never ever lifting her eyes from the floor. Amy had to hear the word 'Yes' as often as poor Jody heard 'No'. They were like mirror images of one another: Amy brimful of the warring desires of her previous minders; Jody at the mercy of her own.

My next safari into the suburbs was to a neo-Georgian estate, to see a lady who fostered young babies for short periods. Unfortunately for the baby I went to see, she had been left there for nineteen months.

'I don't know what the social services are thinking about,' this attractive-looking assistant bank manager's wife told me. 'They know I do short stay only.'

Her way of dealing with her unwanted guest was to leave her in her cot, clean and well fed, but alone, day and night. No affection, no physical contact; as if she were a pet rabbit in a hutch. Her little hands and feet had curled up the wrong way from fear.

'I think she may be spastic,' the woman whispered, 'and maybe mentally defective. She never makes much noise, she just sucks on that piece of blanket. Won't even sit up.' All this without a glimmer of affection or concern.

Hold your tongue Miss Atkins – to show your feelings means you're emotionally unstable. Keep schtumm!

I took little baby Roxanne home, and massaged her limbs until they straightened out. As with Jody, we gave her her own person, the same young girl day and night, but it was a year before we had her running around and two years before she smiled.

So I gathered around me ten such little shipwrecks, all with similar tales to tell. Their problems seemed to me to be only just beginning, not ending, when they came into care. Their parents were more sinned against than sinners, usually girls of sixteen or so, themselves brought up in care, passed like parcels round and round, then falling into the first pair of loving arms to reach out for them and ending up pregnant and alone.

36

I had three young girls to help me: Barbara, who took on Jody, Marilyn for baby Roxanne and Susie who shared the care of the others with me. Oh, and my fully-qualified head prefect, ex-matron of another establishment and a wizard with a bucket, a mop and a bottle of disinfectant, but to my mind only able to frighten the children into submission. She certainly scared me. I sat up stiff-backed at the dinner table like the rest, eating up all my greens, until one day I came home from rehearsals early and caught her thumping little two-year-old Paul, so I chased her out of the house with a mop full of disinfectant, hoist by her own petard!

Oh boy was I in trouble then. Instead of being grateful to me for getting rid of her, Paul, the wicked little devil, took terrible advantage of us all. Holy hell broke loose for a while, plates and cups and knives and tables whizzing past my ears, and many's the time I nearly picked up the phone and said, Come home Ethel, all is forgiven; I'll even buy you a new mop. But we soldiered on, taking a swipe at the odd ear now and again, I must with shame admit, but usually missing.

What I need, I thought, not for the first time in my thirty-five years, is a man, and leaving all the whooping and screeching for a moment I went into the office to telephone the job centre. 'A tame gorilla will do as long as he's got large hands and hates children.' (There's a lot to be said for the iron fist.) As I talked I noticed that the sounds became fainter, suddenly fading away. 'They're all dead,' I gasped, running desperately into the play-room to see what had happened. There they all were, sitting on the floor, while a young man of twenty-two or so, well over six feet tall with a mop of dark red curly hair, sat with them, playing the guitar. They were mesmerised and he was obviously having a good time too. His name was Chris, and he had come to see Susie, or was it Marilyn? Anyway, from then on all I heard from the children was 'Where is Chrissy?' So Chrissy stayed to become my right-hand man, my greatest friend and the most beloved father figure to my children.

Lovers came and went. Lessons were learnt. Once when

weeping over a lost love who had left saying he couldn't put up with me any longer, I was a knowall (who me?), I fell into the arms of a man who helped me out in the office, and who was always lurking about with the odd cup of tea, or packet of aspirins.

'Eh chuck,' he squawked seductively, whipping off his glasses to reveal a pair of wild, lust-filled eyes. 'You know you've always been my pet lamb.'

Hardly the stuff that dreams are made of. Still, any port in a storm I thought; but no, I should have sailed past that port, it was like being washed up in Tangiers. Little Mrs Know-it-all Whitehead was well and truly made a fool of and ripped off. My valuables, such as they were, were stolen and my dignity was badly bruised. A hard lesson that one. Never mix business with pleasure.

After I had been running for about six months, I got a call to go and see the finance department of the county social services. Oh God, what now?

'Miss Atkins,' the dapper, pin-striped head of department came straight to the point. 'What about your fees?'

I should have known there would be a catch in it somewhere. No one was going to let me have all these wonderful children for nothing.

'How much do I owe you?' I queried tentatively. I hate parting with money. Love it. Love it. Love it!

He gazed at me open-mouthed for a moment until a furtive look crept into his eyes.

'Well, actually, we pay you.'

Had my ears deceived me? 'Pardon?'

'A token amount, of course. Just a small payment.' He looked even more furtive as his eyes narrowed and became shifty.

'How much?' I said, looking shiftier yet. This is some kind of wind-up, I thought.

'Er . . . £23,' he mumbled, out-shifting me by a mile.

Oh well, it will help with the coal bills, I thought. Nice gesture.

'Per child, per week,' he went on.

'But that's £230 a week. It's too much,' I blurted out.

Hush up your mouth you fool. He became pompous.

'Well, Miss Atkins, you have to take it, it's the law. And to refuse to accept fees will be contravening Section 4 part 2/43 of the Young Children in Care Act, 1953,' and so on and so forth.

'I'll take it. I'll take it. Oh wow!' I had always reckoned on earning enough money from my acting to pay for us all.

'Light of my life,' I felt like saying and kissing him on both cheeks. But I wonder what sub-section of what Act that would have contravened. When you've got it, flaunt it, baby, flaunt it.

So, with money coming out of my ears, I rushed out and bought bikes and doll's prams and pushchairs then took all the children to Spain for two weeks in our VW bus. Not such a good idea.

Before we had gone a hundred yards someone wanted to go wee wee. Another hundred and somebody else was sick, and before we got five miles from home a riot had broken out in the back. This went on all the way to Tossa de Mar, but it was worth it on the whole. We go back every year, same thing, swearing every year never to do it again.

With two major problems solved – money and a man now for the kids – I was free to set about the real and most important part of it all: getting them better.

They were so different, it was impossible to lump them all together and take care of them in general. Each one had to have special, unique care. Ten little souls in hell. How could I get them out?

Some told me themselves, immediately, by their actions; like Kelly, seven years old, battered and bruised by her natural father, then endlessly rejected by foster parents. Kelly suffered epileptic fits, wetting, soiling and, if left for a moment in the high street, would climb into any pram she saw and curl up in it with the baby. She had been severely punished for this at her last home, but still the compulsion persisted. The answer was so simple; she knew it herself. I took her off all her medication for the fits; it seemed to me they needed dealing with, not postponing. And each day she and I played mummies and babies. I'd put a nappy on her, give her a bottle and rock her up and down in a pram, singing silly songs to make her laugh. We both knew it was only a game, but also an important part of her life she had missed out on and wanted back. It wasn't more than a year or so before she threw the bottle at me one day saying, 'Anyone would think I was a baby or something,' and stalked out of the playroom with her head in the air. No more fits, no more wet beds, ready now to grow up.

Ah, but some were so different. Six-year-old Andrew, fostered with super-respectable folk, one day made the grave mistake of flashing his penis – I've never met a boy who didn't – at his posh foster dad. The family sent him to Coventry. No one spoke to him. When he came into a room, they all left. His meals were put onto the floor for him to eat like an animal, which they all called him. The children of the family had carte blanche to do what they liked with him and after a year of this, his little spirit was broken. Who could survive such cruelty? No spark of joy or spontaneity left. Year after year after year we tried to breathe life back into him, to ignite that little spark of self again. We encouraged him to be naughty and rude and wild, but oh, the damage was so deep and he so frightened to put a foot wrong.

With Amy the damage was deep too, but she was three years younger. I worked so hard. 'What colour are my eyes, Amy?' I would say again and again. But still she looked at the floor. If I cuddled or tickled her, she would stiffen up and laugh a strange high-pitched laugh which had nothing to do with mirth, as if she had learnt it to please me. She sat at the dinner table eating everything that was given to her, filling her little cheeks like a hamster, then chewing slowly through it all, no matter how many times I told her she could leave it if she wanted to. The choice made her more afraid, so I gave her smaller meals, but of course, she would never ask for more. Still the hands had to be washed every half-hour or so; but gradually she allowed me to

40

do it for her, and this was the only time she seemed to relax a bit. A year went by, nearly two, when one lunchtime, as we all sat gobbling away together, a plate came slowly across the dining table towards me and a little voice I didn't recognise whispered, 'I hate meat.' I looked around at everyone. They all had their dinner but Amy. I pushed the plate gently back to her, hardly daring to breathe.

'Do you hate meat, Amy?' She began to shake, but she nodded. 'Then push the plate away again,' I said. She did so. I pushed it back a bit harder. She pushed it back to me and so on until suddenly, with a whoop of joy, she gave it an almighty shove. It spun across the room and ended up sliding down the wall. We all cheered her, hugged her, telling her, 'Well done. Good girl.' (Of course everybody else then had to do the same thing. Dinner everywhere. Come back Mrs Mop!) But she had at last come out of her closet and said: this is me, take it or leave it.

After that she became a fiend from hell for a time, taking her five years of pent-up anger out on me – biting and kicking and smashing and screaming at me, but hugging me tight too and loving me as fiercely. Difficult to tell her from Jody for a time.

Jody still screamed; two years and she seemed as bad as ever. Barbara deserved every medal ever struck for her patience and tenacity, with no rewards it seemed. Jody still recognised no one, wanted only things, not people. Were we doing the wrong thing? Should we just give in and give her what she screamed for?

Not the nicest person in the world, me, at 7.30 in the morning, trying to get eleven children ready for school, most of them refusing to wear what was laid out for them.

'Why has she got pink and I have to wear green? Well I just won't go that's all.'

'What shall I cook you all for breakfast then, kids?' Oh never say that! Whatever one wants, the other ten won't. Every morning screaming like a fishwife, dreaming of the days I lay in bed until two, drinking coffee, smoking an elegant fag, and flipping through a new script.

Ann had a new schoolbag this day and Jody snatched it.

Ann wailed. 'Oh it's not fair. It's not fair. It's not fair.' And I screeched at Jody too: 'You're wicked. Wicked, wicked, wicked.' Whatever happened to tender loving care and understanding?

Jody opened her mouth to begin her scream, then seemed to freeze in time and space, staring at me hard with a deep frown of concentration on her face.

'No!' she said slowly and carefully to me. 'I'm not Wicked, I'm Jody.' And, launching herself from the kitchen step into my arms, she sobbed as if her heart would break, crying, 'Barbara, Barbara, Barbara. I want Barbara.'

She had made it. She was one of us at last; just a mortal. Fear and joy now, not terror and ecstasy. She became totally dependent on Barbara for a while, wouldn't let her out of her sight. Barbara even took her home on her days off.

So, slowly, Jody learnt about love, but it was a long hazardous journey for her, and for us.

Our hyperactive boys, Paul, two, and Michael, six, had to have the world literally slowed down for them. Rushing madly around all day, up all night mostly, we would, whenever we could catch them, rock them slowly backwards and forwards and pat them in time to a soft lullabye. They fought it for ages but it was just too good to resist in the end and gradually they began to come and sit on somebody's knee for a cuddle.

Michael was a budding pyromaniac who had burnt down several garden sheds in his time, so I made him master of the fireplace. It was his job to light all the fires. Oh, but my fingers and toes were crossed sometimes, thinking of the thatched roof. Yet in no time at all we heard the old, 'It's not fair. Why do I always have to light all the fires? Why can't somebody else do it?'

However sweet they all appeared in the daytime, at night everyone without exception grew horns and cloven hoofs: devils sent to torment me and keep me from my fourposter bed. Seldom did I get my head down until way past 2.00 a.m.

I recall one dark day. Barbara had sadly left after four years with us, to marry, and a new girl, Beverley, had begun work that morning. Just the two of us, and me sick with a stomach bug. 'I'll put them to bed,' she said with lively optimism. 'You go and lie down.' An offer I couldn't refuse.

First there was trouble with hyperactive Michael, who kept running into Amy's and Roxanne's room and turning on the lights. They wanted them off. When put to bed by Beverley, he simply screamed and sang at the top of his voice then rushed into the girls' room and turned the lights on again. They both ended up weeping and defeated. Meanwhile, at the other end of the house, the noise had stirred up Jody. Now a real person, it's true, but a very bad, naughty real person, who leapt up and stripped her sister Ann's bed, jumping up and down on it and laughing hysterically. Ann began the wailing, 'It's not fair. It's not fair.' And during all this, Paul, now five, decided he wanted to sleep in the passage, so he dragged his mattress out and lay there smiling and reading the *Beano*, hands behind his head. Screeching and whooping from every corner of the house. I rose from my sick bed, with murder on my mind!

I put the weeping Amy and Roxanne into my room. I then bribed Michael back into his by the promise of a cream-cracker and his light left on, and grabbed Jody, who was by now screaming and swearing, and took her into the garden in desperation. It was a very cold night; it might cool her down.

I told her it was just the night for cursing and swearing, so have a good go then we could all get back to bed. It usually worked. Tonight, though, she seemed to agree with me; said she liked the moon and she would scream all night. We stayed until I began to freeze and, luckily for me, so did she, and she promised to get back into bed and leave Ann alone. So stepping over Paul in the passage once again, I put her down, gave Michael his biscuit, turned on his light, and was just making my way once again to my room, when Paul jumped up, snatched Michael's biscuit and turned his light off. He screamed. Jody leapt up and stripped Ann's bed, Ann began swearing and wailing and Jody laughed hysterically again. Paul lay in the passage munching contentedly on the cream-cracker like a king. Well, I gave what was left of the biscuit back to Michael, put the light back on, dragged Paul, mattress and all, into his room and shouted at Jody – who burst into tears saying I didn't love her – to get back into bed.

'Yes I do, but I don't love what you do sometimes,' I wearily replied, giving her a half-hearted cuddle. Ann then weeps, saying I only love Jody and nobody loves her and, leaping out of bed, hits Jody in the eye. Screams and wails once again from them both. I hold them both down, threatening everything that I can think of – spiders, snakes, you name it.

Suddenly and unbelievably Jody says, 'Oh, I'm tired of all this,' and falls fast asleep. A miracle. Peace in our time.

I go downstairs to console the now weeping Beverley who feels she is a failure and must leave at once, and see my smug twelve-year-old Marcus still watching telly. It's now past midnight. I pack him off to bed. He wakes up Paul and Michael who decide they both want to sleep in the passage. More wailing as I throw them bodily into their beds, take out their lightbulb and lock their door.

'Murderer!' shouts Michael.

'They're all murderers here,' chips in Paul pleasantly.

Kelly's turn now. 'All this noise has made me wet the bed,' she whines. Clean sheets, a bath, clean nightie.

Then I remember Amy and Roxanne alone in my bed. There they sit holding hands with great teardrops rolling down their cheeks because I forgot to kiss them goodnight. I feel like Jack the Ripper.

My last port of call is to my own dear Harry. Propped up in bed, chuckling away to himself while reading of the exploits of his current favourite hero – Annancy the Spider. One thing's for sure, nobody invades Harry's space. Good-natured most of the time, he can be madder than all of them put together if pushed too far. Nobody messes with him.

We share a mug of cocoa and I fall asleep at the end of what was just really another ordinary day, with the knowledge that tomorrow at seven it all begins again and getting them out of bed can sometimes be worse than getting them in.

Occasionally we would get people breezing in, offering to help, but it was help of a doubtful nature. There was the 'gardener' who suffered from agaro- *and* claustrophobia, and spent the whole time in the porch with one foot in the house and one foot out. And the group from Depressives Anonymous who arranged to do some gardening one weekend, feeling that community work for a good cause might cheer them all up.

As fate would have it, a group of bob-a-job boy scouts turned up that very weekend and began tidying the orchard. The depressives arrived and for a while peace reigned. Just the sound of rakes over gravel, lawn mowers and weeds being strangled. Music to my ears; I hate gardening. Suddenly an unpleasant commotion broke out: sounds of angry voices from the orchard. The depressives had met the boy scouts, and rushed to see me in the kitchen.

'We don't feel needed,' they lamented. 'We thought you needed us, and now, oh God, we can't go on!' Choking sobs ensued, perhaps caused by all the cigarette smoke, which now enveloped the kitchen. Ashtrays overflowed. I protested that I did need them, but in vain. Their feelings badly hurt, they trailed out.

'We'll just have to eat our picnic lunch somewhere else,' cried a mournful voice, and the last one to leave turned and said to me accusingly, 'Now you really have depressed me.'

My final glimpse of them was as they pushed their old car over the horizon. Even that was too depressed to start.

A lady gardener I once had took a great shine to me, leaving little posies of flowers and, for reasons best known to her, individual rice puddings everywhere for me to find. Quelle surprise! Well, I took her aside one day and explained that I was horribly normal and only fancied big, butch, muscley fellas.

The sort who whistled at you from building sites. Oh, wrong! After that she took to coming to work in a donkey jacket with Wimpey written all over it, a work helmet and a massive pair of wellington boots. Should have kept my mouth shut.

It all got out of hand one weekend when she invited her girlfriend down. A big girl by any standards: six foot three, ex-Merchant Navy, then a sex change. What a lot of trouble to go to only to end up fancying the same sex. She arrived amid a flurry of white chiffon, wearing a large picture hat, and off we all went for a drink in the local pub where I was greatly admired and respected. Not more than five minutes had elapsed before the girlfriend accused the landlord of making eyes at my gardener and, with a quick flick of her delicately perfumed and bejewelled fist, she laid him out on the bar-room floor. What a scandal!

I took to going in there with the toughest-looking chaps I could find for a while to uphold my reputation as Miss Sexy Drawers 1976.

The gardener simply had to go, which was a pity; her rice puddings have never been equalled.

As with all old houses, there was always something going wrong with ours. The children did their best to help along the process of decay. Every window in the place was smashed weekly. We had a glazier who worked full-time on them, like Sydney Bridge: as soon as he got to one end of the house, he began again from the other end. Beds, tables, wardrobes, kettles, even people, all went through the windows at one time or another, and all latticed too. The cost was horrific. Great holes were gouged out of the walls, and every bit of wallpaper I ever put up was meticulously picked off; poor old Snoopy and the Care Bears and the Wombles, stripped savagely away. Not an ear or a snout left. Not even a whisker. I sometimes thought the children should take up decorating; nobody stripped a wall quicker or more efficiently that they did. I swore each time never, ever,

ever to buy more wallpaper. If they wanted to sleep in pigstyes, so they could. Then next day I was out buying Superman and Spiderwoman. They fared no better. Off with their arms and legs. Off with their heads. I never seemed to learn.

Same with the bedroom furniture. Smashed up to matchsticks within a couple of weeks of being bought. How often did I threaten to let them sleep on mattresses on the bare boards, then forget, and get indignant: 'These poor children's bedrooms are in a mess. They all need new furniture.' Chris and Barbara and the rest of the staff all tried to restrain me but the children were past masters in the art of winding me up over their tragic predicament.

'I come home from school and I haven't even got a chair to sit on.'

'But I saw you hit Andrew over the head this morning with your chair.'

'Yes, I know, but Jody made me do it.'

Endless sobs of tragic despair, so I give in and off we go and buy another chair and the following day someone else gets a wallop with it, and never can a soul be blamed – so many poor innocent victims of cruel fate!

I had my share of four-footed pests as well as the ten large two-footed ones. Rats; pitter-pattering their way round the skirting boards and under the thatch. Party-time every day of the week for them, with all the dinners that went through the windows; all the packets of biscuits smuggled up into the bedrooms, hidden, and forgotten; crusts poked down behind the radiators. They had a field day – but they got a bit too cocky one evening when I sat by the fire and listened as one chewed his way through the skirting-board and right through the log box. When I went to get another log, lo and behold a fat rat, quite unconcerned, sat there washing his ear. One of us has got to go, I thought, and it ain't going to be me; I sent for the rat-catcher. He was there almost before I could put the phone down. Long and thin, with scant pale hair, large ears, small, beady eyes alive with anticipation, and a long quivering nose. He pinned me to the wall with enthusiasm.

'You've 'eard tell of smellin' a rat. Well, I smells rats.' He sniffed the air a couple of times. 'And I smells one in 'ere.'

And with that he was off on all fours, nose a-quiver along the skirting boards, whooping joyfully as he located yet another rat. On catching them (oh why did he do this?) he would insist on pegging the poor dead bodies out on the washing line by their tails. Twenty-seven. His cup of joy ran over.

'Ten shillins,' he shrieked. 'That's what I gets. Ten shillins a tail!'

The children wouldn't speak to me for days. All their friends murdered and pegged out for all the world to see. I was a witch, and what had the rats ever done to me?

I got a dog then to do the dirty work for me, but all he did was herd all the cows in the next field into a tidy shivering group which brought the wrath of the farming gods down on me, with threats of death for the dog and jail for me. He simply wasn't interested in rats; small fry, compared to a fat, intimidated, pregnant Jersey cow.

So then I got a cat. Hopeless. It spent its whole time shivering up a tree with Spotso Charlie the dog sitting underneath, daring it to come down.

Viewed from outside, life at the Crossways must have looked pretty chaotic during the first five years or so. Crash-bang-wallop everywhere. Screaming, wailing, fighting, squabbling. Broken toys littered wherever you looked. Dogs, cats, chickens. Save on eggs, I thought. What a good idea. However, first find your egg in your three acres of garden, and second find it before the children if you want egg on toast, not egg on head.

A goat to keep the grass down: another bright idea which failed. The goat fell in love with Chris. She followed him everywhere like Mary's little lamb, pining when he wasn't there and going right off her staple diet of grass (though still managing to chomp her way through a line full of washing). She had a delightful trick of rushing joyfully to greet you at ninety miles an hour and giving you an affectionate butt in the stomach with her horns, putting you in hospital for three weeks. You took your life in your hands if you set foot outside the back door when she was around.

But through it all I reassured myself with another quotation from my beloved Nietzche: 'Man must have chaos inside him to give birth to a shining star.' Well you better be right, old friend.

I sometimes trembled in the face of so much anger and violence from the children, but I knew in all honesty that it was no good saying to them, 'Tell me how you feel.' It had to be, 'Show me.' Neither could I simply say to them that I loved them; I had to prove it, which meant putting up with them as they were, not as I would wish them to be. They led, I followed. Language was no use. They had already had too many words which had proved useless. You can't eat them or play with them, or even believe them. People can say one thing and mean the opposite. On with the gloves and into the ring. Injustice breeds rage and rage must be discharged, and these children were awash with injustices.

No wonder the hurricanes blew hard and strong through the house and through my life. And how often I failed to see the obvious, dealing unjustly with the rage and stirring up more. There were no miracle cures for their ills. If they were to learn of reason and love I had to teach them by my actions. Me, of all teachers on earth, with my fiery temper, my wild and dangerous mood swings ... I did the best I could and dragged from somewhere deep inside me the magic word: sorry. Hard for me to say, but, if meant, it opened so many doors locked to everything else. And I stuck firm to the silent vow I made each of them when I took them on, that I would never give up on them.

Neither would I ever give any of them up. They had me forever. Ha! Easier said that done. I had reckoned without that jolly old species named social worker. Some, I readily admit, were holy saints and martyrs and as committed to the children's wellbeing as I myself was. But there were others, alas, whose crass ignorance and stupidity left me speechless.

I recall attending the annual meeting for those of us working with and for children in care. The room was abuzz with excitement. Someone had found the lost chord (could it be Snozzle Durante?); the secret of taking care of children's rights once and for all.

The gentleman in question rose to his feet, beard abristle, toes poking saucily through his 'let's all be wild and free' sandals. 'The answer,' he declared, 'is so simple yet so devastating. It will change the face of child care for ever.'

He held a piece of paper high for us all to see.

'A booklet. A simple booklet which we hand to each child as they come into care. It sets out their rights; sets out just what is and what is not allowed to happen to them in care, and the phone number of their local Citizens Advice Bureau for them to ring if they feel those rights have been infringed. I admit it is rather a long booklet – 208 pages in all – but a breakthrough. A major breakthrough.'

The room erupted in roars of delight. Everyone cheered except me, who wanted to ask, 'And can they all live on treacle?' before climbing back into the teapot.

The idea of all those bearded wonders thrusting their booklets into the hands of little frightened, bewildered children, most of whom could neither read nor write, would have been hilarious had I not known from personal experience the devastation their stupidity and ignorance could cause to the tiny people over whose lives they had such power.

Some could easily take all the bullshit in their stride, like nine-year-old Wayne – laid back, streetwise, with a dodger-type cynical half-smile and slow sleepy eyes with which he looked me up and down, approvingly. 'You ain't a bad-looking old bird,' he said at last. Then added, his eyes widening suddenly with surprise, 'Fuck me, look at all them bleeding cows,' as he glanced through the window at the adjoining fields. His bearded social worker, yes, I swear, bearded, who looked as if he were about to go trekking through the foothills of the Himalayas, called Chris and me into the office and said very gravely, 'Wayne here has a serious attitude problem. Five years with this last foster mother and he couldn't learn to love her.'

'She hit me and called me a black bastard,' declared the unrepentant Wayne.

'Ah,' replied his social worker knowingly, giving me the care workers' conspirational wink, 'if only life was that simple. But we know it isn't, don't we, Miss Atkins? I've talked this problem through with my team leaders. We've looked at it from all angles and the answer has suddenly dawned on us all. What a blind fool I was, not to spot it before,' he guffawed merrily, and we all looked at him expectantly. 'It's separation, isn't it? Separation. Loss, mourning, and reparation,' he declared triumphantly, looking round with barely concealed scorn for our ignorance in such matters.

'Mother. He's never separated from his mother.'

'I ain't seen me mother since I was two!'

'That's not the point, Wayne,' he said sadly, shaking his head. 'You don't know it but you're suffering, mourning her loss. You must make reparation. Oh, I'm so excited.' His eyes shone.

Ah, I began to see it at last. He had read his child psychology too. The Reader's Digest version for Neanderthal Man, book one, page one, opening line: 'First catch your child, then talk sensibly to it for a year. After that have it committed quietly to the nearest loony bin as being beyond hope and if you have a brain cell left, commit yourself at the same time.'

But I digress. A meeting was set up for the reluctant pair and mother and son were ordered to meet under the clock on Paddington Station to go through the heady business of mourning and loss.

'Hello then. So you're Wayne, are you?'

'Yeah that's right, and you're my mum.'

'Yeah, that's right.' Long pause. 'So, er, what are we supposed to do now then, Wayne?'

51

'Well I dunno. Something about losing each other in the morning.'

'The morning! You can't stay with me until the bleeding morning. Nothing personal, you understand, but I'm a bit busy. still, I can see what you mean about losing each other in these bleeding crowds. Let's get a cup of tea.' So saying they wend their way to the cafeteria, closely observed by our bearded hero concealed behind a tea urn. Share a cup of tea and a fag, mourn the fact that it's the last one, and Wayne gets the 6.42 train home. Beardy is ecstatic.

'So moving to see them together. So much suffering, so much courage. Hard for me to verbalise the moment.' He drags us all enthusiastically into the office once again and, grabbing paper and pen, draws three circles.

'Now, Wayne, the first circle is your mother, the second circle your father and the third circle is you. You're a satellite. What message would you like to beam down to mother circle?'

'Hey? I'm not a fucking satellite!' The boy looks hopelessly at Chris and me, who are beyond helping anyone.

'It's a game. A game. Now what do you want to say to mother?'

Wayne thinks hard and long.

'Give us another fag!' he exclaims with a sudden joyful burst of inspiration.

'No, no, no!' shrieks the social worker, losing his cool momentarily. 'You're spoiling it all. Spoiling it. For Christ's sake. Oh sorry, sorry, but this is a crucial moment of his life, you see. Now let's try again, Wayne. A father circle. What would we say to father?'

'I'd say, good morning your Majesty!' Beardy gets quite excited. Gives us a now-we're-getting-somewhere look.

'Go on, yes. Why is that?'

'Well see, I think my old man may be Prince Charles.'

'I see. Yes, yes. And what makes you think that?'

'Me mum said she's slept with every sodding bloke in England so I don't see how she could have left him out.'

Game, set and match to Wayne, though the social worker claims the victory.

'He's obviously too overcome by the moment to be coherent. I understand son,' he says, ruffling Wayne's hair. 'It's all too much for you, isn't it? You run along and play now, it's all over.' And, gathering up his papers with smug confidence, he strides out like a man to report all to his colleagues. 'He is free now,' he said as he left us. 'Free to grow up. Make relationships. Free to live. You won't have the same problems his foster mother had. Separation from mother has at last taken place. He may be a little fragile and tearful for a while, which is understandable, so keep an eye on him.' So saying, he was gone.

'Well, I'll certainly try not to hit him and call him a black bastard,' said I, attempting a last shot across his bows. Too late, he was gone. Gone to report to his team, to become a team leader, soon to be promoted to head bullshitter of a whole department. I had endless trouble with Wayne after that. Every time I caught him behind the wash-house having a quiet fag I was reminded that his mother let him smoke, so what right had I to stop him. Who did I think I was anyway? So I smacked him round the ear, and sent for his social worker to share together this new and very significant development. What else?

Andrew's experiences at the hands of these amateur child psychologists was quite a different matter altogether. This time it was the new broom that sweeps clean. A new social worker – a young, eager girl in her early twenties, laden down with files – swept into his life like a breath of fresh air from Sellafield, replacing his previous dear precious one who had turned down endless chances of promotion to remain in the field with her charges, and had fought like a tiger to have Andrew placed with me against all her superiors who had opted for more fostering. She had finally collapsed from nervous exhaustion. The new broom pored over his file with a toothcomb and came up with a juicy piece of information that sent the blood rushing to her pale, humourless face.

'I see. He has had no contact with his natural mother for two years,' she exclaimed. I tried to explain that we left it for the mother to contact him, that way we could be sure she would show up and he wouldn't be hurt. He was still so fragile. His relationship with his mother was a delicate, hothouse affair which needed careful handling. He had been cruelly let down by her before his ghastly experiences with the foster family who treated him like an animal.

No matter how I pleaded his case, she engineered a meeting for them. The best I could do was insist that Chris and I took him. He was so excited, he even allowed me to buy him a new outfit to go in. Usually he would only wear the same old clothes, so as not to stand out and be noticed, but this time we really went to town. He chose everything for himself, even down to his socks, then went round the garden picking the prettiest roses which we made into a posy with ribbons and lace. Oh, God, if you're up there, don't you dare let him get hurt. We set off together singing songs and telling stories and playing I-spy. Mostly to calm my own nerves, I have to admit. But the sun shone, the day looked harmless and Andrew himself was a sweet enough child to delight any mother's heart forever.

On reaching his home town he became more and more excited as he recognised and pointed out places he remembered and, on turning into his road, he suddenly gasped with joy, 'My mother, it's my mother.'

There she was ahead of us, walking up the pavement with her shopping bag. Andrew was out of the car in a flash before I could stop him, running up the road calling, 'Mummy, Mummy, it's me, it's me, here I am, here, here,' and, on reaching her, thrust the bouquet into her hands. She didn't even pause. 'I don't want your fucking flowers or you,' she snarled, throwing them into the gutter, went inside her house and slammed the door. The little boy stood motionless for a moment before turning in his new shiny shoes and running blindly from us down the road, perhaps in the hope that he could run away from it all and pretend it had not happened.

Chris took off after him, whilst I tackled the mother, begging and pleading through the letterbox for her to let him in. It was hopeless, and it broke my heart, so what it must have done to Andrew's was unimaginable. We found him eventually sitting at the top of a children's slide in a playground.

What could we say or do to make it better? He didn't cry or speak or look at us. Just sat there motionless. Let down by us both for setting him up for such a mammoth fall. If I could have died for him at that moment I would have done. I was as guilty as the mother; I was there to protect him from such violence, not to participate in it. No use blaming God or an idiot social worker. I ought to have checked it out first myself, been out of the car before him and standing between them. Sick and disgusted, we drove home in silence. I would say sorry to him later, try to make it better. But this was something that I couldn't sing or hug or pat away. This was going to take time. At least I had plenty of that.

In my early days with the children I was very intimidated by the social services, fearing they would take all the children away from me if I crossed them, but after more than four years I was beginning to feel that maybe after all I had misjudged them. Some of them at least understood what I was trying to do and how long it took to heal all my little wounded soldiers. I could judge how much better and more secure each one was by how far away from me he or she played. At first, wherever I went, so did all of them. Gradually, in ones and twos, they would play outside the kitchen window and by the time they had reached the top lawn three years or so later, we were making progress. But the orchard was the ultimate goal: far and away and mysterious still but full of delights yet to come.

Harry was always fearless and ready to lead them farther afield. He once declared to me on a busy Saturday afternoon that he would take everyone for a walk. Although he was only six he was very sensible, and a walk usually meant into the next field to play on a fallen tree. Okay, I said casually, and didn't give it another thought, until Chris suddenly said, 'Why is it so quiet?'

'They're all playing in the next field.' He looked. They weren't. Neither were they in the field next to that. Perhaps they were in the wood at the top of the hill? So we set off to look. No sign. I was a bit worried now, but not unduly so. We searched the lanes close by. Nothing. Nearly an hour had gone by. We began to panic, ringing up everybody we knew to see if they were there. Eleven children can't just vanish. We called the police, who scoured the roads and the woods and the fields, to no avail. It was beginning to get dark and I was hysteria on legs. Someone had taken them all. It was the only answer, I was sure. Someone in a large van had snatched them up and murdered them. The clock ticked on. Three hours and twenty-nine minutes, and as I looked for the hundredth time across the horizon, I could just make out through the mist several little figures trudging wearily through the long grass. I flew through the meadows, so did Chris, the dog, the cat, the goat and all the chickens (well maybe not all of them!) and there were all my poor weary travellers, munching crisps and sharing a bottle of limeade. Their leader, the intrepid Harry, was wildly indignant that I should have worried. 'I told you I was taking them for a walk,' he said. 'We went to Combe Beacon.' Seven miles away as the crow flies. Well at least he brought them all back, and life went on again as normal.

Having been with us four and a half years, Amy was now a joyful little madam, full of practical jokes and a great mimic. Once, asked how she was getting on by her social worker, she flung herself across the couch, lamenting, 'I feel so persecuted. So goddamn fucking persecuted!' A perfect take-off of a Canadian artist friend of mine who went round London looking like Edith Sitwell then wondered why the police were always picking him up. I got very nervous and agitated when anybody

56

from the DHSS came to inspect me, and Amy wasn't slow to pick this up. She would follow me round the house as I showed the people around, saying, 'It's not usually this tidy you know. She cleaned it all up for you. Oh I see you've got chocolate biscuits with your coffee. Of course, we're not allowed chocolate biscuits. She bought them especially for you. Why have you got your false eyelashes on today, Coral? Ouch, stop pinching me under the table! Oh look, your face has gone all pink.' I would get wild with fury at being cut down to size by her, but it never seemed to make any difference. Anyway who could be angry for long with someone who, sitting by the window one summer evening, looks up at the night sky and says quietly, 'God. How do you make people?' Long pause. And then goes on: 'All right, I'll make it easy for you. What's in my arm?' Another long pause, until I hear her turn away in disgust. 'Huh, well, knickers to God. Doesn't even know what's in my arm.' That, I'm afraid to say, was the end of poor old God. He never got a look in after that.

Jody too was coming on well, nearly seven and at primary school. Her books were beginning to be full of writing and sums; they were hardly ever ripped up or scribbled all over. Seldom now did I have to rush over to the classroom to fetch her home as being beyond the control of anyone there. The teachers even seemed to think she had potential as a scholar.

Her sister Ann had now just begun at big school. Still given to fearful bouts of jealousy, she had nevertheless developed the most delightful sense of humour and could see something funny in most situations, including her own wild envy. But both of them were delicate flowers, needing the security of peace and sameness, and any deviation from this could send them into a panic again, with Jody regressing to a screaming bundle of fury and Ann to ripping and tearing Jody's things.

Well, there was no hurry. I had all the time in the world to get them better. Since my expectations were low, I was always pleasantly surprised, never disappointed. Another ten years perhaps and then maybe they'd both take the world by storm.

FOUR

Nothing could have prepared me for the next bit of savagery. The day dawned happily enough, with the usual squabbles over the unfairness of life. Why me? Why this dress? Why school today? Why sausages? Oh God when will it all end? Yes-sir, indeed. Then into the back of the bus and off, oh joy, to their various places of education, leaving me free for a few hours to clean up after them, make their beds, wash their clothes. Heigh-ho, the white woman's burden.

I was well used to it by now, though I never could say I liked hard work. But a messy house makes me uneasy, too much chaos inside me to cope with it on the outside. So out with the mops and polishes every single day, shining it up like a palace, only to have it destroyed at three minutes past four each afternoon.

It was a blustery March day, and I was returning from the orchard with an armful of early daffodils when the school bus dropped them all off, and I heard their busy little feet on the gravel path rushing round to be the first one to tell me of all the outrages that had been perpetrated upon them that day. Harry once remarked, quite casually, that if you misbehaved at his school, they hit you round the head with a cricket bat.

Shoes, coats, satchels, jam-jars of unmentionable horrors soon littered all my shiny surfaces, and mud was trodden everywhere. All of the children were hot and cross and full of themselves, everyone talking at once, so it took me a while to disentangle myself sufficiently to notice that something was very wrong.

Two somethings: there was no Jody or Ann. Nobody seemed to know anything, only that they hadn't got on the school bus. Frantic with worry I phoned Jody's school first. 'Yes,' replied her teacher, 'we were told you knew, her social worker and two other people took her out of the classroom at dinner-time; she was crying a great deal, but they said it was okay.' The same thing from Ann's teacher: Ann too had been dragged screaming from her lesson by her social worker, who said that it was 'routine' and 'there was no need to let me know'.

I was down to the children's department in a flash. No, I couldn't see the social worker concerned, he was out, so was his teamleader. No one else knew anything and the head of the whole department was out at a meeting and that was that.

Next morning at nine I was there again, ill with anxiety over my two little girls who I knew would be frightened and lost without me. They came clean in the end, sat me down, like an imbecile, and told me a decision had been taken at top level to return the two children to their parents. I hadn't been informed because, 'Quite frankly, Miss Atkins, we believed you would not have co-operated. We feel most sincerely that despite the splendid work you do, you're in danger of caring too much for the children in your charge, becoming too emotionally involved, and in our professional opinion this is not in the child's best interests.'

I burst into tears: Catch 22. Wasn't that exactly what they meant? It seemed the only way to get them back was to pretend not to care over much. In which case, why all the fuss? I never learnt to play this game, giving them instead raw, undiluted me.

I loved those two little girls passionately; I wanted them home, safe with me, and the more I protested, the more convinced became the social workers that they had done the right thing.

The parents had moved out of the area. No one would tell me where they were. I was expected to get on with my life as if they had never existed. The earth began to shake under my feet, bad dreams disturbed my nights, eyes stared and teeth snapped at me from the wardrobe. Panicky and ill, I nevertheless had a house full of children to see to. I must somehow pull myself together and carry on. But after five years together the whole house was stunned and silent, each little child afraid that they might be the next to go. We looked, of course, but where do you begin? As for the parents, their mother had spent most of her adult life in and out of psychiatric hospitals, had had thirty-six sessions of ECT alone, and the last time the girls had been at home for a few hours, their father had chopped up the washing machine with an axe. No, they weren't in safer hands, not by any stretch of the imagination, and my pulse rate rushed up and down, as I thought about them in that crazy wilderness without me. I became anxious and obsessive about the children, needing to know where each one was every second of the day, saw every social worker as a potential enemy, and lived in fear of any stranger who approached the house.

Life did its best to cheer me up. A new lover arrived, descending one day from the sky by hot air balloon, a navigational error, but, oh, love at first sight. He was called Felix. Terribly British and decent and wonderfully rich. 'I'll take you to lunch tomorrow,' he called out as the balloon took off, 'in Bordeaux.' Oh what a spieler! But next day, with a whirring of chopper blades, he arrived once more from the skies, this time by helicopter. We all rushed out thinking it was the second coming, which it was, I suppose, in a way. And I was whisked away from the kitchen sink for a while and into a world where everything was possible. 'How about Acapulco in the spring?' 'Divine, darling.' 'Or a spot of skiing in Les Arcs?' As for Harry, he was becoming a dab hand at looping the loop in the private jet over the Mediterranean.

Everybody got very blasé for a while. 'Send Felix to fetch us with the chopper!' the children would yell as they set off for school, 'and don't bring the spastic wagon!' (the Sunshine coach, which wasn't allowed within five miles of the school, for, as one of the children explained to me with his eight-year-old logic, 'Whenever anyone sees you in one of those buses with all that writing on they know you're a charity child and your friends tease you and people feel sorry for you, and it hurts your feelings. Why can't you paint it out, then no one would know and we'd just be ordinary children?' Oh, what a dilemma. I loved it because I could park it anywhere and never get a ticket!)

Oh, the joy of landing on the lawn at Glyndebourne, complete with picnic hamper from Fortnum and Mason, and sitting through a glorious evening of opera. Felix always dropped off to sleep, but I sat spellbound, captivated by the magic of it all, feeling for a while as Cinderella must have felt when she found the slipper fitted her. It wasn't long, however, before midnight struck for me too, striking him off my list of options.

A millionaire at thirty, Felix lost it all before his thirty-first birthday. No, I didn't spend it, though he was generous to a fault with us all, especially the children. But he had overspeculated, and necessity dictated that he flew off to pastures new to make more. A devastating blow to us high-livers! No more champers on Watership Down! But one has to do what one can, so back to fish-finger sarnies and everybody squeezed into the back of the Deux Chevaux on the school run. Alas now, several years on, the fees I had at first thought so enormous (actually I had discovered they were many times smaller than the going rate: ripped off! Naive little Uriah Heep!) now seemed to go nowhere.

It didn't occur to me to put in for a rise, so we were on skid row practically, despite the fact that I seemed to be working quite a bit on TV. The answer was to take more children, but I refused to do so, keeping Jody's and Ann's room just as they had left it, for the day I found them and fetched them back home. This, despite the fact that nearly a year had gone by and not a word from them; pretty hopeless really, but it just seemed like keeping a light in the window for them, so they might see where they belonged.

* * *

One grey morning, as I flicked through the post – bills, oh my God, how will we live? etc. – I found a grubby postcard which simply said, 'I miss you, Jody', addressed only to Coral, Crossways.

The postmark was a town in Germany. Not knowing what else to do, we phoned the mayor, who luckily spoke very good English, and on hearing of our problem said he felt our best bet was to contact the English army base nearby. The personnel officer there nearly jumped for joy when he heard what I wanted. 'I'm at my wits' end to know what to do with these little girls. Their mother sent them to stay for a week with a relative stationed here, then disappeared: no one can contact her. That was more than five months ago now. We have no choice but to put them into a German children's home.' Chris was away and gone almost before I'd put the phone down, returning next day with our two precious babies, weary and neglected and very, very frightened, both of them, but home.

The other children were so happy to see them, each finding something special of their own to give the girls, to show how happy they were to have them back again. Jody's screams were music to their ears, though she was too terrified for days to move or speak, and just clung on to us for dear life. And we vowed by all the saints and martyrs in heaven and hell never to let it happen to them again.

The social workers were a bit red in the face. 'But mistakes are made sometimes, with the best will in the world, Miss Atkins, and the important thing now is to settle the girls back into school and let them get on with their lives.'

'You bet your lily-livered sweet arses!' I replied, endearing myself to them even more. No one likes to be proved wrong, especially teamleaders in front of their teams.

I asked for an inquiry into how such a devastating mistake could be made. Of course I never got it.

I was tired, disheartened, bitter and angry. The rose-coloured spectacles through which I had at first viewed child care slipped finally from the end of my nose. It would appear that I was impotent to defend my little ones against the mistakes of the social services. No come-back on anyone within their ranks for any of those mistakes, no court of appeal for the children; these people were a law unto themselves.

Jody and Ann were shaken to the core. It took three months of constant loving care to persuade them to return to the classrooms from which they had been so cruelly snatched, and often I had to rush to the schools to collect them early, as they simply couldn't cope.

FIVE

My bad dreams persisted. Strange: I had the girls home, what was the matter with me? Maybe I needed a holiday. I hadn't taken any time off since I'd begun on that June day in 1970. It was now many years later, but actresses, I knew, didn't get tired. We were probably the only people who really wanted to go to work in the morning, who rushed there joyfully.

At first I didn't count my work with the children as work: that was simply being at home out of work. But slowly I began to reverse it all, counting my days in the studios as rest days, and could often be found during rehearsals curled up in an armchair on the set fast asleep, having to be woken by the director to do my scene. This wasn't good enough, I must pull myself together, if only I could sleep at nights. I would wander round the house, looking at all the sleeping children, reassuring myself that they were safe. But once inside my own bedroom, I feared to close my eyes, for the devils that tormented my nights.

I would instead go down and clean the house from top to bottom – anything, rather than sleep – then be so tired the next day I could hardly drag myself around. Once, during an episode of The Sweeney, which was all filmed in five days, no stand-ins, no molly-coddling of the actors, I found myself as the villainess, being pursued by Messrs Waterman and Thaw over some scaffolding, high above London, carrying a case full of loot. I staggered and almost fell off, dropping the case, which opened and spilled all the fake money. Everybody on the ground went tearing around thinking it was their birthday, pennies from heaven! The director was very angry with me, as everything was done by the clock to the minute and I was wasting their valuable time.

I simply wasn't fit to work. So I went to the doctor who gave me some tranquillizers. I took two, but they made me feel worse, with less energy, so I threw them away. No help there. I simply just had to cope. I didn't tell anyone, because what could I say? I'm afraid of the night. I see fierce faces coming at me, teeth snapping; I dream of being a baby rabbit, skinned alive. You're cracking up, you old bag! I thought secretly to myself; a fruitcake!

The show must go on, and I was always on show as a local celebrity, expected to attend many functions, often as the guest of honour.

The annual mayor's ball was a must, since it raised money for my work. I went reluctantly, all togged out like Lana Turner. This year it was being held at the local psychiatric hospital, where the large dining-room was partitioned off with screens to create the right size and atmosphere, and decked out with streamers and balloons, with a big city band playing for us nobs.

The new mayor stepped forward, and introduced himself. 'What an honour, Miss Atkins, such splendid work with all those disturbed little kiddies, you may not believe this but I myself was once disturbed, ho, ho, ho. Of course, I'm much better now.' I looked at his face. Everything twitchable on it was twitching. Oh Lord. 'And this,' he went on, 'is the power behind the throne, so to speak, my lady wife. We call 'er mother.'

Mother stepped forward: everything about her seemed too big, hanging limply, her sash of office appeared to drown her. She shook me tamely by the hand, then, drawing me to one side, whispered sadly, 'I'm not up to this. I'm just not up to it.'

Well, ducky, I know just how you feel, I thought, let's go and find a couple of spare beds.

The dancing commenced. Since I was so famous everybody,

65

it seemed, wanted to dance with me. Passed from hand to hand like a rag doll, doing the mamba and the rumba and the cha-cha-cha. 'I know your face. I've seen you somewhere, I can't quite put me finger on it. 'Ere Alice, who's this?'

'Ooh, I know it, it's on the tip of me tongue, didn't you once work in th' laund'rette at Salford?'

'Madam, how dare you, I'm a telly star.'

What a fickle bunch, already forgetting our heroic Sheila.

'Ah! Y're off the telly, tha's it. Sweeney!'

(Oh, let's not remember that fiasco!)

The ballroom began to swirl before my eyes and I sat down for a moment, snatching up a chocolate eclair and taking a large bite out of one end. The cream shot out of the other end, landing on the floor, just as a ramrod-backed couple were dancing their 'fishtail' past me. They trod on the cream, slipped and fell into the screens, which collapsed like a pack of cards, revealing behind them some of the mentally handicapped children from the hospital, who'd been allowed to peek at us. It was all too much for them. On seeing all the food and the balloons they gave a whoop of delight and leapt into the throng.

Utter chaos, with the mayor wailing, 'Order! Order! I must 'ave order! Mother'll 'ave another bloody nervous breakdown!' And mother's voice was the last one I heard as I made a hasty retreat, lamenting, 'I'm not up to this, I'm just not up to it.'

Well, there's always someone worse off than you, I comforted myself, as I wove my way home, with howling wolves and flaming dragons looming up at me from the headlights of the car. Maybe I should turn back and book myself in.

Or perhaps it was the season for dragons in the Thames Valley at this time of year.

Next day I had to go to a reception in the town hall, where the local councillors and the mental health authority were meeting to applaud my work in the community.

'Coral Atkins, a steadfast, stalwart, strong, invincible and unshakeable inspiration to us all,' boomed out the chief bigwig, and I wanted to snatch him by the lapels and holler, 'Ya gotta help me, doc, I'm crackin' up! Don't move back! The world ends two feet behind you, I can see it tailing off.' Instead, I smiled my stiff little smile, and declined the proffered glass of champagne.

What else could I do? My hands were shaking so much I would have spilt it all over him. 'Have to keep a clear head,' I joked, as the floor began to slope away from me, and I edged up to the door handle and clung on to it for dear life.

Overtired, that was it, just a bit overtired. I talked to Harry's dad, Peter, who suggested I come to France for a week, where he was shooting a film with the artist Nikki de St Phalle, in a medieval castle in the Languedoc. It sounded wonderful.

Chris and the others said they would hold the fort, so Harry and I set off. It was certainly a beautiful place, unchanged, I would say, since the fourteen hundreds. Even the plates and goblets were old pewter, and the beds all original oak four-posters with tapestries still hanging round them, and the grounds rambling and wild, marred only by several large statues, all the same, some twelve feet high, placed at intervals everywhere. Tall and cylindrical, they were rather like rockets with strange heads on the top. I began speculating on what they could be when I was cut short by my seven-year-old son: 'They're giant willies, Coral, don't be silly.'

Er, yes, so they were. Well, I was a passenger on this trip, and as the film crew buzzed around me, I lay in my bikini in the sun, ignoring the omnipresent phallic symbols as best I could, even using them to shade me from the noonday heat.

I began to doze off, but was rudely woken by a princess from Greece, leaping over me on a black horse, pursued by an army of actors dressed as surrealistic beasts from Hades, howling and wailing, their horses' hooves missing my little nose by inches. I moved away to what I hoped was a more secluded spot, under a hedge, and did manage to sleep, only to be woken this time by someone kissing me up the inside of my leg. 'Let me gaze at your child's body,' he murmured in a thick French accent, like Pépé Le Phew. 'All day long I paint the machine, how I love the machine, you are like a beautiful machine, I must 'ave you,' and so saying threw himself upon me.

'Uurgh! Get off me you ghastly, hairy horror!'

'I will make such love to you, you will never be the same again.'

He meant business. Never have I come so close to being raped. I had to use every ounce of strength, both physical and verbal, to get him off me. Once he realised I too meant business and would have none of him, he shook his head sadly with genuine feeling.

'Oh, I feel so sorry for you, you 'ave missed something wonderful,' and still shaking his head in mystification, he left me.

Same thing every day, everywhere I lay my weary head, something or someone sprang out of the bushes at me, snatching at my arms or legs or ears or eyebrows. I think the film had stirred them all up. It was very sexy, all about nuns, naked from the head down, painted all over with psychedelic snakes and butterflies, being ravished by the actors dressed as animals, in a chapel, in front of a, yes, you've guessed it, man-sized penis in a coffin, bollocks and all (and you madam).

They were having a whale of a time, except the poor actress whose artist lover it was who'd taken such a shine to me. He pursued me over hill and dale on his little short muscley legs, his long hairy arms and big hands everywhere. It was about as restful as being on safari with David Bellamy.

What happened to the bike rides of my fantasies, laden down with armfuls of wild flowers, picnics in the middle of cornfields, poppies twined in my hair, chuckling knowingly with my golden companions about aspects of Proust's fifteen-volume novel? There had been nothing in my dreams about my being seen as a piece of spare crumpet, which is about what it amounted to.

It was worse at night, when I was fair game for all, in my

oak-panelled bed with its dusty drapes. Dust and spiders everywhere as I fought for my virtue, finally dragging my covers into Pete's bedroom in order to sleep. Unfortunately, he had his very neurotic and jealous American girlfriend with him, who, on seeing me enter, rushed out into the night, wailing like some Trojan woman who had just learnt that Troy had been razed to the ground and her children lost. Well, I thought ungraciously, I hope she falls in the moat then I can have her bed. I was knackered.

The next day was the last straw. As I lay nodding off against one of the penises, they all blew up like a twenty-one-gun salute, the climax, dare I say, of the film: man's final act of defiance against his horrible predicament. 'One small wank for man, one huge wank for mankind,' boomed the loudspeakers, and I snatched up Harry, who was having the time of his life helping Peter film all this, and fled off home.

So much for the arts. I'd had it with actors, writers, film directors, and mad balloonists. What I needed, perhaps, was a straightforward, ordinary man from one of the respectable professions to take care of me, teach me how to live a nice, quiet, ordinary life. Surrounded daily by crazy wild children, I needed to be lulled to sleep at night in the arms of normality. Of course!

I looked around to see what was on offer. Who would want mad old me with all these kids? Well, someone did: a Jewish accountant from Milton Keynes; youngish, handsome, very respectable, with his own thriving business, a flat, a car, a chandelier and lots of uncles in Manchester, whom I was rushed off to meet on our second date. 'But is this a serious union, what are your plans for our boy? *You* are after all a shiksa; pardon! but it must be faced, we're worried you see, so worried!' I tweaked their whiskers, and reassured them as best I could that I had nothing but honourable intentions towards their shining light.

And that was true. I wanted to be normal and do what normal people do. 'Have you had a good day at the office dear?'

'Oi vey! Have I had a good day she asks! A good day today! I was only served boeuf en croûte with beans and chips! Can you believe it! Beans and chips! Nothing so bad has ever happened to me. Heads must roll! Heads must roll!'

Well, I'll never ask that again, er, but what's boeuf en croûte? Never mind, out with the recipe books, whipping up the odd soufflé. I'm very fond of beans and chips actually, especially in a sandwich, but I guess all those bad old ways will have to go . . .

He certainly lulled me to sleep at night, so safe in his arms, as he watched over me, literally. I would fall asleep with him propped up on one elbow gazing adoringly at me, and wake nine hours later to find him still in the same position, his great brown eyes gazing unblinkingly into mine. Nice and safe, mmm, goody. A bit, well, unnerving really, but better than having one of them blacked which seemed more like normal to me.

Oh, how far removed from reality I'd become, ordinary people were nice and kind and loved you.

'Morning, darling,' I would murmur.

'Yes!' he would reply, in an anguished cry wrenched from his soul, 'but do you love me? I *must know*!'

Sweet!

'I'll have two boiled eggs today, not one, and lots of buttered toast and yes, coffee, not tea, coffee. Fresh, mind!'

Ha! This is the life that I've been missing, I thought as he rushed in with the laden tray. I cracked open my egg. 'Tut, tut, this egg is too hard. I can't eat a hard egg.'

'I'm sorry, sorry, Oh God, God I'm sorry! I'll get you some more, but *do you love me?*'

How could I not love him, no one had ever brought me breakfast in bed. '*But for Christ's sake get it right!*'

'Better?' He holds his breath as I take a bite.

'Mmmm, but now the fucking toast's gone cold.'

His flat was nice and ordinary too, all blacks and greys and chromes, with posters of aeroplanes and aftershave ads, giving it just the right touch of class. Neat and tidy, everything in its

Presenting paintings
to the Royal Academy
at the age of fourteen,
with my friend
Maggie Dawson.
(Keystone Press Agency)

Oh how lovely it was to be me, going on eighteen and unstoppable!

Peter Whitehead: as deadly as a rattlesnake to this little country mouse.

The earth stopped turning and our son, Harry Dominic Whitehead, came into the world.

Fame at last, with the cast of *A Family at War*. *(Granada T.V.)*

Older, but no wiser, in *Flesh and Blood*.

Glenda Jackson –
generous to a fault.

My parents helped,
though they thought me
mad too.

A vain attempt to clear
up the garden at
Crossways. *(Photographer:
Chris Ware of Keystone
Press Agency Limited)*

Seldom did I get my head down before 2.00 a.m.

Chrissy and me with some of our angels.

A goat to keep the grass down – not such a good idea.

All hot and cross from school.

Three of my girls, grown up now and so beautiful.

The Crossways, 1971

Gyde House, 1989

Harry and his mom, summer 1989.

Sylvia, mother and me collecting mother's poetry award in the USA, 1989.

place: socks in the sock drawer, hankies in the hankie drawer, shirts all neatly starched and stacked on shelves, and his suits all hanging tidily with the lightest one end, darkest at the other, shoes shining and trendy, all with shoe trees in them. So different from my own house at Hoe Benham, which seemed to have a fine coating of Instant Whip over everything.

Mr Wonderful. My only regret was that the children didn't seem to see him through my eyes. I only took him there a few times, as a lot of sniggering went on, and some open hostility. Someone flicked a spoonful of trifle at his nice new suit. I was furious. Well, of course, he was right, I was working too hard and needed time for myself, away from them all, and at his flat. So I spent every Saturday night to Sunday evening there.

Harry came too. With me it was always love me, love my son (and buy him lots of presents, and turn your office into a bedroom for him, because he simply must have his own room).

'Of course! God you're right! How selfish! What do I need an office at home for?'

Harry did really well.

He liked his breakfast in bed, too, with croissants and a cream cake from the local delicatessen. 'Oh and see if you can get me a copy of this week's *Beezer*, and a packet of Smarties!'

'Oh and darling – '

'What darling?'

'You haven't forgotten you promised to take him to the zoo this afternoon, after you've cleaned out my car and cooked the lunch?'

Here's to the nice normal man in the street! So why did I sometimes get this terrible urge to scrunch up all his shirts, and fling them in the air? And mix up his socks and his pants? And why did I almost pass out each time he put a clean hanky in his pocket? 'Never leave home without one.' Why did I try and force him to go out without a hanky, till one day he nearly had an epileptic fit? He simply was incapable of leaving the house without a clean hanky. I must face it. And what's so wrong with that anyway? It is perfectly ordinary. The fact that I wiped my nose on the back of my sleeve just showed how sick I was.

He had two little toys that had come through his childhood unscathed, Pinky and Ponky, who had pride of place on his pillow. I took an instant dislike to them, so smug and clean, how dare they come through thirty-three years without a mark on them? What kind of child would allow it? I hung them both, once, from the chandelier.

'Yes! You see how ill you are now my darling, you need rest! Rest! And peace and quiet, and do you still love me, I *must know*!'

'Yes! We all must know! We're so worried!' echoed the whole family.

'So sick. So worried!'

He cut the two toys down. I'll get you some other time, I thought, as he placed them neatly back on the bed. And next I rolled them up in puff pastry and stuffed them in the oven. Bears en croûte. Yummy yummy.

Then I put the chip pan on.

'She's crazy!' screeched his mother, holding up the two charred bears. 'She needs locking up!' (She never did like me, can't think why.)

'No, no, no!' wailed her son. 'It's love she needs! More love! More endless love!'

And the uncles opted for the proper diet and good fresh air, a spin in the sports car, perhaps, to blow away the cobwebs.

'But where! Oh God! Where!' agonised the accountant. 'What do you want to do, and where would you like to go? Tell me! Tell us all! We must know!'

What was where, where was what, which ... what? ... where? 'Ipswich!' The best I could come up with, as they all peered down at me. I had just had a plateful of beans and chips and all I wanted to do really was sleep. But I was whisked away with the warm wind in my hair, in the vague direction of Ipswich, Harry reading a comic in the back.

'How much?'

'What?'

'How much do you love me?'

'Ah . . . lots.'

Nice one, good.

The car screeches to a halt. 'Lots of what? You could mean lots of nothing! That's no answer!'

'Lots of . . . um . . . pomegranates.'

'Ah I like that, that's good. Lots and lots of pomegranates.'

'Heaps.'

'Heaps! I like it!'

We set off again, brmm, brmm, brmm, through the lovely country lanes, lady's smocks and cuckoo pints and warm spring grasses filling the hedgerows. We stop again abruptly.

'No! I won't buy that! What kind of answer is pomegranates? You take me for a fool! I asked a simple question! How much do you love me?'

Desperation creeps into my voice. 'More than the last time you asked me.'

'How much more?'

'Ah . . . two hundred million gold ingots more.' We'd be taking off into outer space soon.

'Gold ingots. Oh!' He thinks about it. 'Yes!' he smiles. 'More like it, much more like it.'

Off we go again, brmm brmm brmm, screech to a halt again immediately. 'No! Look, I just don't get this,' he argues. 'What kind of love is gold ingots?'

A little hand suddenly smacks him hard round the ear.

'Put a sock in it!' says a furious Harry. 'I've had enough!'

That was too much for the accountant. He wails to the heavens. 'Smacked round the ear by the boy I've treated like my own son! Haven't I done everything for you? Given you everything! Wasn't I gonna have you barmitzvahed on your thirteenth birthday, even though your mother's a shiksa?! What – God?! What do I do wrong? Give it to me straight, God, let me have it right between the eyes!'

'I'm going for a pee,' says Harry, giving him a withering look of disgust.

'I'm coming with you,' say I, giving him the same withering look.

We hopped out of the car, and squeezed through a hole in the hedge. Once through, with a quick glance at each other, we made a run for it. Over the hills and far away, laughing and shouting and rolling in the long grass, like a couple of old lags who've just gone over the wall at the Scrubs. Endless love tried to follow, of course, but his high-heeled boots were barely made for walking, let alone running over hill and dale, and his Engelbert Humperdink suit left little room for violent movement.

'Why?! God! Why?!' echoed the lofty skies, as we sped on. 'I must know why.'

Too late, my fine plump little bladder of lard, the birds have flown.

We bought some strawberries, and sat on a deserted railway station in the hot sun munching away happily, unable to look at each other for laughing. Then we hopped onto the first train to arrive and chugged merrily off in the wrong direction. Who cares, because I remembered for a while what I so easily forget, that happiness equals Harry Whitehead!

Oh how good it was to get home to the wildness of the children, the mad-eyed goat sitting cross-legged by the fire, the chickens perched on the kitchen window-ledge demanding their dinner, passion and fury flowing like the sweetest wine through each living thing in my life there. Even the weeds appeared like orchids to us, as we two weary travellers returned from what seemed like another planet.

And so ended my preoccupation with normality. He was normal all right, a nice normal obsessional neurotic with paranoid delusions, to my mind. And if I imagined his preoccupation with me would end so easily, I'd reckoned without the four-and-a-half-thousand-year endurance test of his race. I have always loved the Jewish people: I wore a Star of David long before I met him as a mark of respect for their suffering in general and for their individual acts of generosity towards me since I took on the children.

He, I knew, would be a headcase, whatever race he came from. But oh the tenacity, like a terrier with a bone. He would not let go. First the phone calls, day and night, pleading, whining, cajoling, bribing, threatening; desperate visits at midnight; weeping scenes of misery all over the furniture. Amy re-enacted it for me the next day, didn't miss a phrase, a gesture or an intonation. Then came the old 'I'll kill myself' chestnut, and when that didn't work, things took a sinister turn for the worse.

I was proud of my children. Jody and Ann had been back for ten months now. Ann had found a friend, whom she brought home from school. A real step forward.

Amy, though finding reading difficult, was a wizard at cards and could do any jigsaw puzzle upside down. Andrew had thrown a chair at me one breakfast time – well done, attaboy – and Harry filled my heart with joy.

When he was six, I'd been asked to remove him from the village school, as he did his work in five minutes then spent fifty-five minutes distracting the class. So I sent him to a prep school, where he won a scholarship which paid his fees at a posh public school. 'Hello Mumsy!' I hoped he would say as he skipped out of school, but alas it was always, 'Watcha, Atkins.'

My oldest boy, Marcus, was bringing home the most beautiful pieces of carved furniture that he'd made at woodwork. And Michael and Paul, my two little bundles of furious quicksilver, walked sometimes now, instead of running, and even stopped to build things, not just to knock them down. One of my youngest girls, just starting school, was very fragile, and was having a hard time being bullied. She suffered all kind of cruel name-calling because of her colour.

'Wash me hard in the bath tonight, Coral, and get it all off.'

Oh, so heartbreaking. I told her stories of places where everyone was golden like her and where I would be called names, and I said I would take her there one day. 'But I don't want them to laugh at you,' she wept, 'it hurts so much.'

What to do? Only one way out. I invited all the teasers home to tea, making such a huge fuss of them that they all left feeling like kings and queens, wanting always to be her friend and come home with her. Best I could come up with, and it wasn't long before they loved her for her own sake. One of the boys had problems too, but oh, did he turn the tables one day. Slowly, slowly, catchee monkey. Take your time, all will be revealed! What a child. From being bullied and thumped, and teased and humiliated, he rose slowly like a phoenix from the ashes.

Kelly, who used to hop in and out of prams, now hopped on and off horses, jumping three-barred gates, and bossing us all about at home like an old mother-hen.

And my last little girl to arrive, Joanna, was finding her own way of surviving. The oldest of a family of seven, it had been her job to take care of all the new babies that appeared, being left in charge of two tiny ones when she was only three, and getting severely beaten and whipped if she put a foot wrong. So hurt and lost herself, she nevertheless was a smart cookie who somehow had immense power over the other children and always ended up with their new toys. 'Look what Jo gave me!' would cry an ecstatic Jody, holding up an old tin can.

'What did you give her in exchange?' I would ask.

'Oh nothing much, only that new dolly that I had for my birthday.'

Not bad, eh?

Jo's bedroom was filled from floor to ceiling with teddies, dolls' prams, pushchairs, cribs, large dollies, smaller dollies, new dresses if they fitted her, the best bedlinen, the newest quilt covers, and all done with such innocent charm, it was impossible to scold her, for, as she would say, 'I didn't make them give it to me, they wanted to.' Well, she sometimes resorted to pinching and squeezing, but she did it so quickly you could never see anything except the bruises she left behind. It all indicated to me the vast emptiness she felt inside, and her panic that no one would be able to fill it for her, so she had to do it for herself. She too had her fragile side, sometimes climbing into bed with me, the tears rolling silently down her cheeks, unable to tell me what was hurting her, and not daring to allow herself to be comforted by me. Then after about an hour she would just go quietly back to bed without a word.

Sometimes she left me drawings under the pillow of a little girl and a lady in front of a neat brick house on a lovely sunny day; only problem was, she always drew a tiny witch on a broomstick in one corner.

She seemed to have some kind of rapport with Harry. She never tried to get his things, and would sometimes confide her fears to him, although he was two years younger than she.

One night he let me know, in confidence, that he would be sleeping in her room because she was afraid that there was something behind the curtains. I went to bed quite late that night, and was just about to turn the light out when a little figure came creeping into the room. Harry sat on the bed, paused, and then said quite casually, 'She's asleep now.'

'Good,' I said. There was a pause.

'I think she may be right, Coral. I think there is something hiding behind her curtains.'

I thought about it for a bit. 'Well maybe if she's asleep, it would be okay for you to sleep with me now.' He hopped quickly into bed and turned out the light.

Lots of tossing and turning and sighing until he finally sat up and put the light back on again.

'No, it's no good, I'll have to go back. Supposing she wakes up, she'll be so afraid.'

'Shall I come with you, Harry?'

He thought for a long moment, his manhood hanging in the balance . . . then got quickly out of bed. 'No,' he said at last, 'I have to do this by myself.'

I felt shamed, my own night terrors fading into insignificance at the thought of this seven-year-old keeping watch over the sleeping Joanna, and standing sentinel between her and whatever horrors waited for them both behind the dark drapes in her room.

So many of the children were capable at times of shocking me into silence with their individual acts of generosity.

We once had a thirteen-year-old called Martin staying with us for a while; a very damaged boy, just about hanging on to his marbles by the skin of his teeth. His case history, too complex for even me to understand, read like a street map of Marrakesh — so many twists and turns and cul-de-sacs. He suffered, not surprisingly, from massive epileptic fits, and I dreaded the first one, fearing my children's reaction to it.

I needn't have worried. As I was cooking in the kitchen one afternoon, Jody rushed in, asked for a warm flannel, then rushed off again.

Better see what she's up to, I thought. Well there she was, Martin on the floor, a fit in full flood, his head resting in Amy's lap as Jody wiped his face and Andrew held him down. And afterwards, when it was all over, sweet little Amy stroked his hair, and said, 'Don't be afraid we won't love you if you have fits, because we will, we don't mind at all,' and everyone agreed. Kelly brought him tea and toast.

I think to myself at moments like that, 'I'll never get mad with them again.' Oh yes, of course, I always do, they weren't always so generous and understanding of his funny little ways. He was a great flasher for a start, which was okay at home: 'Oh put it away, Martin, we've seen better things on Sainsbury's meat counter!' His laugh, too, which was so piercing and demoniacal it made me want to rush for the nearest nuclear fallout shelter, could almost be contained indoors, and also his preoccupation with neurosurgery. But when all three were put together, in the town, he'd go too far.

The children would give him a lecture before we left home, no flashing or laughing, or singing about surgery.

Alas, the warnings so often fell on deaf ears, and in the middle of the park he would have a quick flash, laugh like the devil himself, then shin up a tree and sing 'The Lord is my brain surgeon!' at the top of his voice. 'Oh just keep walking, Coral, and pretend he's not with us!' I was sorely tempted to do just that.

But I tried hard to hang on to him. He was brilliantly good at chess, and now and again I felt he understood what I was saying, and retained a little of it. But I rashly made the big mistake of promising to come and fetch him, wherever he was, if he ever ran away, which he often did – to the local village or the town, no big deal.

Unfortunately, the more I fetched him back, the harder he tested me, often ending up in far-flung exotic places like Ashton-under-Lyme, Grimsby and even Aberdeen. The phone would ring. Oh God, Martin, where now? My toes, fingers and eyes crossed in silent prayer. 'I'm in, just a minute, I'll spell the letters.' He couldn't read. 'B-A-', oh, let it be Bath! let it be Bath! 'N-' (No) 'G-' (NO!) 'O-R.' (Oh *hell*! Talk about promising more than you can deliver).

'Listen to me Martin. Can you hear me? Now listen. Can you see a policeman? Go and find a policeman, give him this phone number, and ask him to – *Martin! Mar . . .!*'

'No, I'm at the railway station, and I'm staying here until you fetch me like you promised.'

Down would go the phone, and that was that.

Chris and I took it in turns to collect him, using whatever old wreck-on-wheels we happened to own at the time, a miracle that they made it to the end of the drive let alone to the corners of the universe.

But what choice did we have? It went on like this for a year, until the social workers decided he'd be better off locked up. I'm not so sure. He was carted off to the John Donne Behavioural Modification Unit at a mental hospital in the Midlands (do I hear poor old J.D. turn in his grave?), where he literally had to sing for his supper.

They had a token system there, each child earning their evening meal with tokens for good behaviour. If they didn't have enough tokens, they got food supplements – drinks with vitamins in them.

Poor little Martin, who didn't even know what the word behaviour meant, let alone being capable of differentiating between good and bad. I tried to spring him, of course, but the hospital hung on. With fees in the region of one thousand pounds per week, who can blame them.

I personally think he would have been better off taking his chances with us, and on the open road; at least he got a good meal at the end of his travels, and a cuddle.

SIX

Well, I couldn't have sung for my supper either, Martin, not if my life depended on it. I was slipping and sliding through the days, shivering through each night, certain I was being watched from every corner of the bedroom, and through the windows too.

This was actually true now. I'd discovered that my jilted lover had taken a turn for the worse. He'd sold his mother's house and moved her in with him – a certifiable act in itself. He'd even got rid of his business and the Roller, and was spending all his money on an army of private detectives to follow my every boring move.

Sometimes I could swear I saw them all in the tall pine trees, disguised as rooks, calling to me on the warm evening air. 'But do you still love him? We're worried, you see, so worried! And we all must know! Owwh owwh oowwh knowww!'

On one occasion, I spent a pleasant evening with a casual acquaintance, an army colonel friend of Felix, decent chap and all that, who talked mostly about landscape gardening, of which he was a great exponent, and told me all the wonderful things I could do with my garden. We chatted happily as we drove home to his cottage for after-dinner coffee.

As he stepped out of the car, he was roughly grabbed from behind by a large Darth Vader look-alike. My mad-eyed accountant appeared from nowhere and began wailing, 'What's between you two! Come on, I can take it! Give it to me now!

Let me have it straight!' Then making a grab at me, he wailed, 'How? How? How?! I ask myself! How?! Why?! With him! Oh God! What did I do?!'

You get the idea.

I, too terrified to do the decent thing, leapt back into my friend's car and drove off like a bat out of hell, leaving him to his fate. When the chips are down, it's every man for himself. As I screeched away, I heard him yell, 'Pull yourself together man! This is just not cricket! Ouch! I'll put you on a charge!'

What a cringing coward I was. I slept under the bed that night with shovels and spades and a poker, but he stayed away. My poor friend forgave me – women and children first, of course – but he had been forced to listen to four hours of whining before he could convince the accountant that we were not even just good friends.

I could do without all this. Weren't things bad enough inside my head? I was finding a me I didn't know at all, a person who was afraid to look at the sheep in the fields, who had to block her ears at night, to cut out the sound of the birds singing in the early morning. To catch even a few notes of their song would have me weeping uncontrollably with grief.

'How can ye chant, ye little birds, while I sae weary, full of care?' Why was I so full of care, so fragile, so panicky, so restless and afraid? No, not of the accountant; real problems have real solutions. I was afraid of nothing but natural things, like cornfields and trees, and now black cats. Oh Mother. God, gentle Jesus, someone, help me.

Perhaps the new production I was about to begin would make a difference. I was to play Titania in *A Midsummer Night's Dream* with Robert Powell as Oberon and Ben Kingsley playing Puck, and the whole of the Covent Garden Opera singing Purcell's 'The Fairie Queen' to accompany us.

It was paradise. The rehearsals went well, the actors were loving and friendly and brilliantly clever, and I began to lose myself in the magic of it all. The music lifted the play even beyond its own measures of perfection.

The weekend before we opened, I went home to be with the children. I was happy and high, as only an actress can be on the brink of what must surely be the most magnificent experience of her professional life. The children seemed to shine with joy too, knitted at last into a real family.

I took them out for the day. We walked on the downs, marvelled at the mysterious Avebury stones and picnicked on the left hoof of the White Horse at Uffington, then returned home to supper and a warm summer fire, round which we all sat telling each other ghost stories, shivering and clinging together. Ha! but no ghost could get us; we had each other, we were safe.

Nobody heard the car turn into the drive. The dog barked a couple of times, well he was always barking at shadows, we took no notice. But when there was a sharp knocking on the back door, we had to stir ourselves. Probably someone bringing old clothes or toys. People often did on a Sunday.

Andrew opened the door. 'Four people to see you, Coral.'

'Oh well.' I disentangled myself from the now sleepy Roxanne and Jody, and went to see what fate had brought this lucky and so blessed family on this fine summer evening . . .

Fate isn't always kind. There on the back porch stood Jody's and Ann's social worker with three official-looking strangers, waving a piece of paper in my face.

'We've come for the girls,' they said. 'They're placed with you under Section One of the Young Persons in Care Act, which gives neither you nor us full parental rights. Their parents want them back, and we're here to see that they get them. Please fetch their things, and don't try and obstruct us, we can get a court order.'

I looked back into the living room where Ann was fast asleep in Chris's arms, and Jody and Roxanne were curled up together on the couch like two kittens; hard to see where one began and the other ended.

What should I do? What *could* I do? Stay calm, Coral, calm. Don't frighten the children. Don't scream. Don't punch these strange intruders in the face because you'll only make things worse.

Sweet Jesus, oh sweet Jesus, what had I promised these two little girls the last time it had happened? 'Never! No, I'll *never* let it happen to you again!'

'Please,' I began to weep, 'please I beg you. Not today, not now. I'll do anything you say but not now, not this way. Let me prepare them.'

'Hide them, you mean,' said one angrily.

'No, I won't. I promised them. I gave them my word this would never happen to them again. Can't you see that? You must listen to me!'

'Miss Atkins. We're used to you and your devious ways. Now don't waste our time. The quicker it's done, the better for everyone concerned.'

We had kept our voices low for I had no wish to alarm the children, but they soon seemed to pick up the scent of my fear, and in ones and twos gravitated slowly towards the back door. Not in their usual noisily curious way but quietly, as if they too knew that something really bad was about to happen.

'Show me the paper,' I demanded of the social worker. Well, of course, it was in order; no loopholes there. What if I ran off with the girls now while these people packed their things upstairs in their bedroom? Oh, but then I might lose all my children.

The whole house seemed to hold its breath for a moment as we stood either side of the back porch sizing each other up, before the spell was broken by Jody, who had made her sleepy way to the back door and, on seeing her social worker, began to scream. This was the cue for everyone. Total panic broke out, the children crying and clinging to me for dear life. Oh how hopeless, my sweet little babies. I can't save you from Mr Wolf. And so I stood helplessly by as Jody and Ann were marched upstairs, their clothes and toys roughly thrown into two black plastic rubbish sacks. Then the girls were dragged screaming from my arms into a waiting car. As it pulled off down the drive, their little tear-stained faces pressed up against the back window, I too began to scream. 'Jody! Jody! Let me know where you are. Send me a card. Jody, I'll get you back. I'll come for you, I promise! I promise!' I screamed, as I chased after the car. It screeched away into the night and, for the first time in my life, I passed quietly out in the driveway like Elizabeth Barrett Browning and was carried indoors by Chris.

Fainting is one thing; coming round from a faint quite another. At first I panicked, not knowing who I was and thinking I was shut up in a woodshed. Then, as I began to remember, I panicked again at what had just occurred. Chris, Marion and Alan, who had all been with me for many years now, loved the children dearly too, and were almost as bad as me. We took care of each other as best we could, all of us sleeping in the sitting room that night, cuddling up to the children and helping to soothe their nightmares – and our own.

'Ill met by moonlight, proud Titania.' The following afternoon I had a dress rehearsal and in the evening a first night. What a joke! Where's your music now, Purcell, to soothe my troubled slumbers? Your magic potions, Oberon, to make everything all right again? And how was this shattered wreck of a woman going to put on the mantle of majesty and transport an audience into a fairy land she knew was peopled only with devils?

Well, I got myself to the theatre somehow and, once dressed up in all my finery, nothing of the real-life drama I was caught up in seemed to show. Just the odd trickle of perspiration tracing its way through the make-up. I don't remember the first performance. The stage does strange things to an actress. Once on, the collective years of responsibility to the play seem to take over and carry you triumphantly through. It was well received. The critics actually seemed to think I was good. A mad-eyed queen, powerless to save even herself let alone her subjects. I got through the second, third and fourth nights too, but waking on the morning of the fifth, knew something was terribly wrong with me. The bed was wringing wet for a start, my hair matted with sweat, but, more than that, I didn't seem to know who I was, believing myself to be in a huge high bed with only the birds' dawn chorus for company. This, of course, had me shaking with sobs and I was afraid to move, thinking that some fearful thing was in the bed beside me.

As always, I pulled myself together eventually and slowly the real day dawned: the play tonight, and breakfast now with the other actors – nothing to be afraid of. I dressed and tidied myself up as best I could and made my way down to the hotel dining-room. Everyone was there, sweet and friendly as usual, all calling out greetings to me.

'Good morning,' I replied, then froze. No sound at all from my voice. Silence. I tried again. Nothing. Oh God what was happening to me?

The cast were very kind. They could see I was ill, and a doctor was called for. I had a high fever and an infection of the larynx and must stay in bed for at least ten days. No! I had to go on tonight! Give me something to bring my voice back and I'll be all right. I had never missed a performance in the whole of my career. Life couldn't be this cruel to me and take me out of the production, surely? I sent for a specialist who said the same thing: I was too ill to work and might lose my voice forever if I tried to force it. Lucky day for my understudy, but for me, home with my fairy wings clipped and a broken heart.

My own doctor could find nothing physically wrong with me. 'Nervous exhaustion, Coral, I'm afraid. You'll have to take things easy for a while.' 'Yes,' I croaked. 'Yes, this time I really will try.' And I did. The children were off to Spain for the annual Ride of the Valkyries in the minibus and I had decided to stay home this time and rest. Put my dainty feet up on something and cherish my poor battered spirit. My sister Sylvie, who lived close by, had agreed to come over and help me clean up the house and the two of us stood peacefully in the drive, waving to my departing family and planning how to spend two quiet weeks together, when the phone rang.

'Is that you?'

'Who?'

'You, what's-your-name. The one who ruined my life, killed my husband, lost my son his business and lost our home. Mind you, nothing against you personally you understand, you're a nice girl, but he's got a gun and he's coming to kill you.'

Help! The accountant's mother. I'd completely forgotten about him!

'A gun, you say?'

'Yes, a gun. You'd better get out quick. I don't want him in jail for the rest of his life over a floosie like you. Run!'

This doesn't happen in the Thames Valley in July. This is rubbish. Hysterics. My sister and I look at each other, laugh, then, panicking, rush upstairs and hastily pack me a suitcase. Leaving it in the hallway, I set off to change out of my nightshirt when, with the screeching of brakes, an old battered car pulls up and out jumps my crazed lover. Without a second thought, Sylvie shoves me into the broom cupboard and, leaning casually against it, says quietly, 'Is anything wrong?'

What an understatement! With eyes staring from his head and an ugly and very suspicious bulge in his jacket pocket, he snatches hold of her. 'Where is she? You've got to give it to me straight. You've got to let me have it right down the line. I've got to end it. I can't go on. It's finished. I'm going to finish us both!'

'Who? Me and you?'

'No. Me and her.'

My sister breathes a sigh of relief. 'Well, you're too late. She's just left for Spain with the kids.'

'Oh no, no, I don't believe it! Oh God, oh no, what now?' he weeps, sitting himself down on my suitcase.

Sylvie then does a curious thing. Setting up the ironing board in front of the cupboard, she drapes a sheet over it and begins ironing. I later learnt that my toes were poking out from under the cupboard door. Smart thinking! It takes the accountant a moment or two to realise what he's sitting on but when he does, he shrieks again: 'It's hers. This is her case. She'd never leave without her clothes. She's still here and I'm staying until she turns up.'

Checkmate. Well, almost.

'Have a cup of coffee at least,' pleads my wily sister, lacing it heavily with sleeping pills and, as he slowly nods off, arms round all my clothes, I take off for the airport in my nightie and bare feet. Who cares? Never have I been so scared.

When the children arrive in Tossa, they find a half-naked, shaking, quaking jellyfish waiting for them. Just what the doctor ordered! Sun, sea, sand and five of us to a room. At the end of two weeks I'd had it. My doctor ordered me to a clinic where I was to be put to sleep for a week. 'Anything you say. Anything at all.' No fight left in me, I meekly put myself in his hands.

Oh the shame I felt at throwing in the towel. 'Don't let anybody find out for God's sake.' The local press would love it. They were always looking for things to write about me. One week, in desperation, the local rag's headlines shouted: 'Actress, Mother of Eleven, Pays Parking Fine.' They'd have a field day with actress, mother of eleven, goes bananas and is carted away to loony bin!

'It's a private clinic, Coral. A private clinic, not a loony bin.' Same difference to me. Total defeat and despair and disgust. Sylvie and I set off for Harrow and she did such a good job on me on the journey that I was beginning to look forward to the rest and the lack of responsibility by the time we reached there. I almost bounded out of the car and up to the plush reception desk where fate had one more little treat in store for me.

As I reached over to shake the admission doctor's hand and sign in, I caught sight of a small figure sitting in a large leather armchair by the window: the accountant. Oh my God. With a shriek of 'He's got a gun and he's going to kill me!' I rushed madly off into the grounds, lots of white-coated figures in hot pursuit. Do they carry tranquillizing darts up their stethoscopes?

'This case is worse than I at first suspected,' muses the head shrink, who has been convinced by this time by the accountant that I am a raving nut and he's my loving, worried husband. 'Such a nice, reasonable boy.'

'He's off his chump. You must see that!'

'Ah, you see how ill she is,' pleads the accountant. 'Let me have her. Hand her over to my care. I'll soon sort her out.'

You bet. One swift bullet to the temporal lobe.

'Me? Hurt her? Kill her? Carry a gun? You see what I mean?'

Oh Sylvie, why didn't you stay to explain? It takes me ages to convince the clinic that it's him not me who should be locked up. I don't believe they ever were convinced, but to humour me they got rid of him in the end. What a fine start to a week of peace and quiet, and I never did find out how he knew where I was going. I believe he must have had the phones tapped. He was so devious anything was possible with him. I never knew for sure whether he was carrying a gun. All I knew was that he scared the hell out of me.

Well, I'm popped into bed eventually with sweet Eurasian nurses to fuss over me and kindly doctors hanging on my every word. Woken twice a day to be bathed and fed and talked to, then glorious, miraculous, blessed, blessed sleep again and after five days of this I'm woken up and sent to talk to the consultant psychiatrist. I felt so foolish. What could I say? We sat there for a while in silence. What does one say to a shrink anyway? Can't really say, 'Nice weather we're having for this time of the year', can you? But can you say, 'I'm afraid of my dreams. I'm a baby rabbit lying on a bed of wet straw, its stomach ripped open, slowly dying, being watched over by a huge, indifferent woman in a massive pinafore'? No, I can't tell anyone that.

'You look frightened, Coral. What's so frightening I wonder?'

The tears begin to run down my cheeks. No one has ever noticed that before. 'I'm just being silly. There's nothing to be afraid of, is there?'

'Oh, I'm not so sure. Perhaps you're right to be afraid.'

That did it. I began to spill the dreaded beans of all my terrors of the night and he didn't laugh or make me feel foolish. At the end of the session, he asked me if I'd ever wondered why I had opened a children's home in the first place, and why I knew so much about disturbed children: something that had never even crossed my mind before. 'Well, I was never a disturbed child. That's for sure! I had a lovely mother and father and nothing bad has ever happened to me,' came my quick reply. So why did I begin suddenly to shake, my teeth to chatter?

I had four more sessions with him before it was time to leave the clinic, and had, by then, to face the fact that all was not as it seemed or as I would have wished it to be in my dim past. Skeletons, as yet unmasked, lurked by the score there.

The consultant seemed to take a great shine to me, as I poured out my ideas on the children and how to get them well. He suggested that I too would one day make a fine psychotherapist. 'But it will mean years of personal therapy which may turn your world around, Coral. Are you up to it?'

'You bet. I'm up to anything,' I replied boldly through wildly chattering teeth. No point in being chased through my life by shadows. Better to see them out in the open, however bad they were.

Well, then I was kicked out of Paradise. 'Oh let me stay another day. An hour. A few minutes!' I even sank so low as to dip the thermometer into my early morning cup of tea. 'See! I'm ill! I've got a high temperature now!' Only problem was, the tea was so hot that the mercury shot right out of the other end. Still, the rest had done me good, and I certainly felt a little stronger, and before I left it was agreed I would write a thesis and present it to the Guild of Psychotherapists for consideration. If they liked it, and me, chances were they would take me on and train me to be an analytical psychotherapist. I trembled at the thought. 'I don't know anything about mental illness,' I protested to the psychiatrist. 'Yes you do. Take your time. Write about the children.'

The children. I thought hard and long. Amy; not as she was now, but as she had been when she first came to me. I remembered my reading then in Winnicott about schizophrenia. The fragmentation of the integrity. Wasn't that exactly what was happening to sweet, precious Amy? Her lack of spontaneity; the fearful, ritualistic washing; her false little laugh to please me, and the phrases repeated again and again: 'I'm a good girl. A clean girl. A quiet girl.' All learnt parrot-fashion as a way of surviving in a hostile, threatening world of conflicting demands. Needing constantly to adapt and re-adapt to survive it. Nobody wanted the real little girl who came to life only when she screamed and wailed in terror. Who would give that girl houseroom? So she hid it as best she could. So clever. To my mind a perfectly normal reaction to a totally abnormal world, where the lunatic foster mothers had taken over the neat little semi-detached asylums. Ah, but the truth was lurking there, in her refusal to look me in the eye. She knew in her heart it was all a sham and feared I might see it too.

What would have become of her if it had gone on? Would she have adapted once too often, splitting as it were the very centre of her self and, like the atom, letting out nothing but chaos, leaving her at the mercy of her own creation: lost forever on some back ward of a mental hospital? It didn't bear thinking about. Too terrible to ponder.

Was that all schizophrenia was, then? No more than people playing Russian roulette with children's minds before they were old enough to have any certainty within them to fall back on? We shall see. Far too simplistic, I thought nervously as I packed up my notes ready to send.

I also added a bit about my observations on epilepsy. All the children with it I had come across, responded to physical handling, and all had one thing in common: they had been wrapped up tightly as tiny babies and left for long periods. Could it be a baby's way of panicking? And, once the mechanism had been set in motion, rather like hiccoughs, hard to stop? One thing I found, for sure: that medication was only a substitute for twenty-four-hour tender loving care, and I wouldn't consider it. All of the children responded and got over their fits; even Martin, who was having five or so fits a day when he came to us, had maybe one a month when he left us after a year. The important thing seemed to be to keep your eye constantly on the child and know when their anxiety was building up in order to allay it with tenderness, cuddling, just gentle patting and singing – anything soothing and diverting.

I felt very foolish and naive as I sent it all off to be scrutinised by the experts. What an idiot, they would probably think, and such a childish way of putting things. I might as well forget it. It was no more than a good exercise, and though I watched eagerly for each post, I had little hope of a favourable reply.

However, the gods sometimes smile on the foolish, and I was invited to present myself to the training committee. Oh Lord, something else to get het up about. Worse than going for an audition at the National. And what on earth did one wear to see a bunch of psychotherapists? No matter. Whoever I came as, they'd see through it!

As it happened, I needn't have worried at all. I had two long interviews and they were all wonderful to me. Kindly and so interested in my observations on the children. No sniggering. No savage questions to frighten or outfox me and, at the end of it all, they were in agreement that I was a suitable case for training. Wow! Like a dog with two tails I sashayed home to tell everybody that I was now going to be a real smart-arse and they would all have to watch out!

Well … it's not quite that easy to become a smart-arse psychotherapist. First you have to read your way through the collected works of Freud, Jung, Klein – ugh! (I threw Klein's book on the psychoanalysis of children across the room then stamped on it. What a load of rubbish!) – Greenson, Fairbairn, good old Winnicott and a whole host of others I'd never even heard of before. And the seminars were at first very intimidating to me. No one seemed to use simple words like love, fear, joy, sadness but talked instead of narcissistic phallic pre-Oedipal levels, primary object relations and the pathogenesis of neurosis. Help! And quite a few of the women students used their hands a great deal; talked about caring, sharing, empathy and holding.

Well don't hold me, I thought, and was very glad I had been given a cynical old Nietzschean scholar as a therapist for myself!

The course was a four-year one consisting of one weekly seminar, two sessions per week with a supervisor and a tutor, case discussions with members of the training committee, together with, after six months, clinical work with a training patient of my own and, of course, most important really, my own personal therapy twice weekly for the whole course.

I couldn't think what I could say to somebody twice weekly for four years, but there was no choice and, to be honest, although the week in the clinic had helped, my nightly horrors were as real and ever-present as always. Anxiety and restlessness stripped me of all my natural energy for my dear children who still needed so much loving attention, and little Harry had nothing but a worn-out wreck for a mother.

I was glad that my therapist liked Nietzsche, so that I was able to confess that I kept a copy of *Thus Spake Zarathustra* by my bed, rather like some people keep the Bible, to save my soul when all else failed. And he understood! He understood! The first step towards gaining my confidence. I tried so hard to be open and honest and to lay bare my hidden unconscious for his scrutiny, but the unconscious has a life force all its own, rather like a little wild animal, who, no matter how you coax it, won't trust you until it *can* trust you. There are no short cuts.

The years had gone by, nearly three, when, after a very bad and restless night, I entered his consulting room and gasped in amazement: 'You've got new curtains. Lovely, new, red curtains!' They shone and they gleamed at me.

'Yes, Coral, they are red, but they've been there ever since you first came.'

Oh how frightened I was. I would have sworn on all I held dear that they were greeny-grey; hadn't I been lying looking at them twice a week for years? I should know. I began to shake like never before.

Red. What was it about red? 'I'm so afraid! So afraid!' I stuttered, reaching out blindly for my therapist's hand.

'What's frightening you, Coral?'

'The wolf,' I heard myself screaming. 'I'm afraid of the wolf.'

Thirty-nine years old and scared of wolves. What was the world coming to? But come hell or high water, wolf, whoever you are, I'm coming to get you before you get me, however high the price. I won't allow you any longer to keep me from the colours of the rainbow. Take my hand, Mr Therapist, and together we'll go a-hunting wolves.

SEVEN

The little girl's eyes shone with joy as she looked through the windows of the old Morris 8 at the streets of London slowly giving way to fields and trees, with flowers sometimes in the hedgerows. The seaside! Maybe she was really going to the seaside at last!

She was only three and didn't actually know what the seaside was, but her sister Sylvie, who was nearly six, had been there last year with her grandma and had told her the seaside was the very best place on earth. She chuckled gleefully, jumping up and down on her mother's lap in excitement at the thought.

Her mother and father had been very secretive as they packed up her and her sister's things into a large brown suitcase. No matter how many times she'd asked they simply wouldn't say where they were taking her, which made her sure it was some really, really wonderful surprise. They had even allowed her to bring her doll Rosemary in a pushchair – something she had never been able to do before.

The car sped on. Mile after mile of winding country lanes, the little girl's excitement soon turning into sleepy yawns and, before long, she was so fast asleep she didn't hear the car draw up outside a run-down old farmhouse on the edge of a wood in the middle of the Dorset countryside. Her mother woke her gently.

'We're here,' she whispered, sadly, it seemed to the child, but with a whoop of joy she leapt from the car and on seeing a field of waving corn nearby, rushed into the middle of it crying, 'Is this the seaside? Is this really the seaside?'

'Don't be stupid,' growled her sister, and everyone else laughed, but she herself felt she had never seen anything so beautiful in her whole life. She'd been brought up in a place called Tooting, in London, where there were only pavements and sometimes a park. Nothing like this!

'Come and meet Mrs Lewis,' her mother called to her from the house as her father began unpacking the car. The child was of an age when, still being passionately involved in her immediate family, she had little interest in strangers and, to be truthful, they made her anxious. But, keen to do her mother's bidding, she shyly pushed open the heavy old farmhouse door, and entered the kitchen. It seemed huge to her, with a cold stone floor, a large table in the centre and, along one wall, the biggest fire she had ever seen with two huge black oven doors, one on each side.

Where had she seen something like that? In a picture. That was it. The witch in *Hansel and Gretel* had a fire just like it. Edging closer to her mother, she at last looked up at the old woman sitting in a big wooden chair by the fire. This was the strangest-looking woman she had ever seen: big as a house, with iron-grey hair growing low onto her forehead and held captive by a black hairnet. A massive pinafore covered her frame, and she wore a great pair of men's slippers on her feet.

'Say hullo to Mrs Lewis,' urged her mother, pushing her gently forward. 'Granny Lewis,' chuckled the old lady, 'everyone calls me Granny Lewis.' And, lifting her bulky frame from the chair, she swept the child high in the air in her arms. 'Give old granny a kiss then.'

Ugh! This wasn't nice at all, thought the little girl, stiffening up and trying to keep away as the huge face planted a giant kiss on her cheek. And she's got hairs on her chin! Well she won't be allowed to touch Coral Rosemary again! The old woman laughed. 'Ha! She'll soon get used to me, don't you worry. They all do in the end. I've got five placed with me now. Little devils they be but I soon sorts 'em out.'

The talk went on. Something about all the men being gone and no one to cut the corn now. The child was glad, as she skipped out into the sunshine once more, to take her doll into the middle of the tall corn stalks and tell her all about the horrid old lady who smelt bad, with hairs on her chin and how, if you looked hard, you could find red and yellow flowers in the seaside. So engrossed was she in her game that she didn't notice the warm October sunshine giving way to a chill, cold evening wind.

Looking round once, she thought she saw her beloved mother standing on the edge of the field watching her. Were there tears in her eyes? No, thought the little girl, it's just sunshine. She waved her posy of wild flowers and asked her doll Rosemary if perhaps they could spare a few for her mother's hair, like a daisy chain.

When at last the chill wind pierced her cardigan, she knew it was time to go in so, wheeling her pushchair, she set off in search of her parents. The dark was all right but only if mother was there to make it so.

First she looked into the kitchen, but saw only her sister curled up in a chair, a big hanky held up to her face as she quietly sobbed. She'd probably been stung by a bee. She herself had been stung once and it was a terrible thing. 'Did a bee sting you, Sylvie?' she called.

'It's Mummy and Daddy,' sobbed her sister. 'They've gone.' The child's heart missed a beat. No! Wrong! Her sister was wrong!

Rushing outside again, she called to them, feeling sure she would see the old car where they had left it. Just an empty space. She thought hard. A game! That was it. Hide and seek. Her daddy often played silly games, sometimes hiding the car round a corner till she screamed and shouted for him in joyful terror. All she had to do was look.

It was really quite dark by now, but her fear for her parents overcame her own feelings of unease. She knew only too well what happened to people if you didn't find them, like the girl in the song about the Mistletoe Bough who had hidden in a trunk in the attic on her wedding day and no one could find her so she died. She must find her mother, before something like that happened to her! She called out again and again as she peered in all the old barns and outhouses. Nothing! Oh nothing! Must she really face the dark wood now?

Her panic rising, she stood on the edge screaming out her mother's name till she was grabbed roughly from behind and carried into the kitchen. The big room seemed to spin. Where was safe? Everything here was strange and unfamiliar, the big oven doors looming large and fearful, and the cold stone floor seeming to sway and swim before her eyes. Dimly she saw some other children around the kitchen table. Big, wild children, eight years old at least.

'I want my mummy,' said the little girl bravely. 'I want my mummy now please.' The old woman let out a laugh. 'She's long gone. There's only old Granny Lewis to take care of you now. Come and have a little cuddle.' The child backed away, shaking her head. Something about this woman was more frightening than the loneliness. 'I don't like you,' she replied honestly. 'I want my own mummy.'

The other children shrieked with laughter at this, and the old woman began shouting and swearing at them, frightening the little girl almost beyond her reason. As she looked wildly around the room, she at last saw something safe: her pushchair and, making a rush at it, she clung on to the metal handles as if her life depended upon it, her little body shaking with fear as her screams broke the silence.

All the king's horses and all the king's men, or so it seemed to the child, tried to prise her fingers from the pram, but so tightly did she cling on that it felt to her that they would have to break her fingers first before she would let go. Fear has a power all its own, but it was no match for the forces against her and eventually she was wrenched away, carried roughly upstairs and thrown onto the biggest, highest bed she had ever seen.

'We'll see who likes who,' growled the old woman as she stomped out of the room and down the stairs, leaving the child alone in the darkness and the silence. Her cries continued for some long time, eventually giving way to choking sobs and shuddering sighs, her whole body seeming to scream out for her mother's touch: the mother from whom she had never been more than a few minutes away since the day she was born.

How could such terrible things happen? Where was the sense in it? She knew bad things happened to you when you were asleep because they had happened to her before but always in the morning when the birds sang there would be her mother's sweet face smiling down at her and everything would be better. Maybe that was it. Maybe if she could sleep until the birds came she would be safe again.

This was a terrible bed. She tried rolling into the middle to get warm and comfy, but it was wet and cold there and it smelt bad. So, crawling as close to the edge as she could get, and curling her legs up tight under her to avoid the damp, she fell into a troubled sleep in which she dreamt of her sister, red paint, the smell of linseed oil and her father's voice. 'Skin a rabbit alive,' he would say, as he stripped her clothes over her head to pop her into the bath. Skin a rabbit alive.

Maybe if some other noise had woken her in the morning it wouldn't have been so bad. A loud bang, perhaps: a clap of thunder; or maybe someone stomping into the room. But it was the joyful optimistic chorus of the Devonshire birds that first pierced her troubled sleep. The birds. She stretched luxuriously. Another lovely day beginning, she thought, keeping her eyes tightly shut to savour the moment. Maybe we can take the dog Judy to the park today.

The second thing to happen on this strange morning was her feet touching cold wet sheets, and her outstretched arm feeling a large warm body next to her. Opening her eyes suddenly, she was at first completely lost, all memories wiped out until, with a rush of grief and despair, the events of the previous day came back, flooding through her little body like a tidal wave, feeling for a while as though it would wash her away forever. Her mother was gone, and she was alone in this fearful place, and the birds hadn't brought her mother back.

Perhaps she would have drowned then in her misery and despair had it not been for a sharp punch in the ribs, bringing her quickly back into the present, and an angry voice demanding that she shut up and keep still.

She looked fearfully in the direction of the voice: oh help! The bed was brimful of children: a big girl and some dangerous looking boys all curled up together. How dreadful! Oh how dreadful! She scrambled quickly out of the covers and dropped to the floor, shivering there on the cold lino in fear. What else was there? How could she save herself? She must think.

The game! That was it! Everything was going to be all right because it was only a long, long game of hide and seek, and all she had to do was find her mother in that dark wood and all would be well again.

Feeling round in the dim light from the blacked-out window, she at last located her shoes and, popping them on quickly, she let herself out of the room as quietly as she could, down the steep stairs and, with a quick glance at the old woman's chair which was now empty, she was out into the chill morning air and away.

The wood didn't seem nearly so frightening in the daytime. There were birds singing and some flowers too, and filled with a giddy, feverish optimism, she rushed from tree to tree. 'Mummy, I give in. Mummy, are you there?' she called. So many trees, so many brambles, but she knew she must search behind each one as, if her mother was truly locked in a trunk like the song said, she wouldn't hear her calling.

The day grew warm, with shafts of sunlight piercing the tall trees leaving warm patches on the grass and, after a time, as most small children are able to do despite their fears, she curled up on one of the patches and slept.

This time, she dreamt of a book with pictures of a dark forest, a cottage and her sister inside twirling and dancing as she often did, in a bright red cloak.

She woke with a start. The sun had vanished, and great shadows were covering everything. No hope today. 'I'll come again tomorrow, Mummy,' she shouted, 'I won't give up.' She felt hot and ill, despite the coldness of the evening, and was glad to see the lights from the cottage although it offered little comfort. At least she could curl up on the floor somewhere, maybe, and sleep.

The old woman seemed cross with her, and was saying something about her being drenched in sweat. It meant little to the child who was grateful this time to be carried up the stairs and dropped onto the bed where she lay for several days, drifting in and out of consciousness, the events of the past two days jumbled up in her mind like a recurring nightmare.

As she was able to think more clearly, she began to recall the events of the night before she came. Her daddy painted pictures, and this time he was painting one of her sister Sylvia in a red cloak with dark trees round her and shadows, and when she had asked him what the picture was about, he had read to her from a big book a story about a little girl called Red Riding Hood who had gone to see her granny in the middle of a dark forest. When she got there, the big bad wolf had eaten her granny, put on her clothes and was pretending to be a kind granny to the little girl. 'What big eyes you have, Granny! What big teeth!'

'All the better to eat you with.'

What did it mean, and why had her daddy told her that? Her only experience of life outside of the family was what she learnt from books, as real to her as her own house and toys. Was her daddy trying to warn her, perhaps, of where she was being taken? She thought hard about the old woman. Not very nice. Not very nice at all. Smelt bad and growled, with hairs on her chin. And the big oven doors: were they in the same story too? She couldn't be sure. How to find out? How to be certain?

She trembled now, each time the woman came near her, fearing to look in her face lest she saw teeth and large eyes gazing back at her, oh she must look for her mummy again. As soon as she was able, she slipped once more out of bed in the early morning light, stopping this time to search the deserted kitchen. Not many places to hide. A table, chairs, sideboard and little else. Just a door she hadn't noticed before. With faint hope, she pushed it quietly open, unable at first to make out anything in the gloom. As her eyes adjusted to the light, she thought she made out a pair of eyes looking back at her.

'Mummy, is that you? Is that really you!' she called out joyfully. Receiving no reply, she crept into the gloom, then stopped in horror. A pig was staring down at her from the shelf. Not a whole pig, just his poor head.

Rushing out of the pantry, she squeezed herself under the sideboard and lay there trembling and gasping for breath. She knew now; she knew for certain. This was a wicked wolf she was living with and she knew all about him, and this must be the piggy who built his house of straw. Oh foolish piggy! She caught you and ate most of you up. 'Little pigs, little pigs, let me come in, or by the hairs on my chinny chin chin'. . . It was all true! And maybe the oven doors were where she'd cooked him. Who was next? Did she eat little girls too? Of course she did. If she ate pigs, she'd eat anyone.

All of the stories she had heard from the safety of her father's arms were now coming true, and she was all alone with no one to help her handle them. How did the children with the oven doors stay alive? What happened to Little Red Riding Hood? She wished now she'd listened more intently. Something about not eating and poking a stick through the bars. Well, she could do that. And she thought that the daddy had rushed in and chopped up the wicked wolf and they had all lived happily ever afterwards. Is that where her daddy had gone then? Home to get the axe? No wonder he took so long. It was far, far away to London. If she could stay alive until he got back, he would soon make an end of this wolf forever. She had never read anywhere that wolves ate mothers. She must still be in the wood waiting to be found.

So, with a sigh of resignation, the child began to squeeze herself out from under the sideboard when, with a noise like Jack the Giant Killer, the woman's feet came into view, banging backwards and forwards across the kitchen floor. All she could see were feet, ankles and the end of the pinny, but it was enough to force her once again to brace herself against the cold stone floor.

'Breakfast,' called the wolf woman at last, and the children came clattering down the stairs with groans of 'not porridge again, and no milk nor sugar'. Fattening them up for the pot, thought the child in horror, longing to rush out and warn them, but lacking both courage and language. Soon they were gone, the old woman went up the stairs again and the little girl was free to continue her desperate search.

And so it went on, day after day. Her panic sometimes got the better of her, forcing her to scream out her mother's name to the lonely tangled wood. Sometimes she slept on the cool, damp grass, then went home to the horror of the evening meal, never being sure whether it was her turn to be popped into the oven or boiled like the poor pig's head and served up for supper.

The misery she suffered at the hands of the older children in that big, high bed paled into insignificance in the face of her daily struggle to save her own life. It's true the children once hurt her so badly she cried out, but it only brought the old woman up with a stick, with which she beat all the children savagely, including herself. She never cried out again whatever they did. Her sister Sylvie sometimes tried to defend her against the bullying, but she herself was only six and no match for the others. 'Leave my sister alone,' she would say, which, though it had no effect, was a comfort somehow to the little girl, and made her feel cared for.

A day once dawned when everybody was nice to her, the big girl dressed her in a clean frock and the old woman making her a rabbit-shaped blancmange. 'It's your birthday,' they all said, 'you're four.' The child screamed then, rushing round and round the kitchen in a panic. It couldn't be true! She was three, she knew she was, and if her mother came back to find her she wouldn't know her if she was four, and no way was she going to eat a poor rabbit painted pink.

She rushed out of the house and crouched miserably behind the rainwater barrel, trying to work it all out in her mind when the unimaginable happened. An old Morris 8 turned into the drive and there were her precious mother and father laughing and crying and hugging her, with sweets and cakes. Now you'll see, she thought. Now you'll see you wicked old wolf. But where was the axe? Where was the murderous anger against these people who had hurt and frightened her so?

She watched in speechless horror as her mother kissed the wolf and her father shook her hand and gave her money, then, after giving sweets to all the bad children, they were into their car and about to drive away. 'Don't leave us!' screamed her sister. 'She's wicked! She beats us! Oh please, please take me with you! Take me with you!' But the car had gone, leaving the two little sisters once again to face the snarling wolf alone.

Now she really did snarl. 'I'll give you wicked,' she yelled, grabbing the little girl's sister by the roots of her hair and dragging her inside. 'I'll show you what a beating really means.' And with a fury unseen till then, she began hitting the child again and again round the face and head with the full weight of her anger. Her sister rushed round and round the kitchen in a vain attempt to find somewhere to hide but found nothing better than the table, under which she crouched shivering and screaming, blood now pouring from her nose, covering her arms and hands as she tried to fend off the blows.

'My sister! Not my sister!' screamed the four-year-old over and over again, but immediately the woman turned on her. 'You want some of the same?' she yelled. 'Then get out! Go on, get out now.' The child stood on the threshold of the room, her love for her dear sister battling with her fear for her own life, and with a sob the fear won and she threw herself face down on the dusty gravel path in a frenzy of despair. The wolf was going to kill her sister and she had done nothing to save her. How could she ever in the whole of her life make it up to Sylvie for leaving her there under that kitchen table screaming all alone?

Her sister didn't die, but to the child she might as well have done. Sylvie was no longer the wicked, furious demon of before, but good and obedient, eager and willing always to help the wolf in any way she could, and it frightened the little girl to see this. Everyone she loved was gone now. The two people in the car she was certain were wolves too. No real parents would have behaved so; she had never read it anywhere. They simply wore masks to make them look like Mummy and Daddy, as she wore a gas mask and it made her look like Mickey Mouse. She must never trust them and must keep out of their way.

What had become of her real mother, she wondered, as she sat amongst the tall corn once again, no longer to play but to conceal herself from attack; unable now to see the pretty flowers that had so delighted her a year ago, the colours all faded into a greeny-grey mist of misery. She was dead of course, and the child knew nothing of dead mothers.

There was a story once about a poor boy, dirty as she herself was, who had no mother either. He was called the Lost Boy who went up chimneys and he had found the place where all dead mothers go by jumping into a dark river. She remembered the picture of it. Well there was one like that at the bottom of the lane. Perhaps she should go and see.

It was a fast-flowing stream, dark and mysterious with green weeds and white pebbles at the bottom, and she searched it diligently for any sign of the lost boys or their mothers. You had to jump in and go right under, she knew, and wept for she lacked the courage. She sat there day after day, dropping stones in now and again in the hope of attracting her mother's attention: sometimes she called out her name hoping maybe she would leap out as sometimes a silver fish did, and snatch her

105

little weeping daughter into her arms and take her to the place of all lost mothers and their children.

It wasn't to be, and soon she forgot why she went there. The river lost its meaning, as did many of the things that she had once taken for granted and delighted in. Even her name was forgotten: she knew it had a 'c' and an 'o' and would sometimes be found scratching furiously on the ground with a stick: CO, CO – but soon she forgot how to join up the 'o', and the 'c' lost its meaning too. She was always called 'you' by the woman and the other children, so that's who she thought she was. Just a 'you'; loving no one and loved by no one and fearing everything, with nobody now to interpret the world for her as a safe place in which to live and play.

The name of the game was staying alive until bedtime, and staying silent until morning: everything else was ashes. Even the remains of her doll Rosemary, which she had discovered in the wood shed, though it filled her with sorrow somehow, forcing silent tears to drop onto her grubby hands, couldn't stir her memory of a Paradise once hers alone and now lost.

The days and weeks became months; the little girl withdrew more and more into her silent sorrowful world, asking for nothing, needing nothing; the only signs of life the large teardrops which sometimes fell, unnoticed, from her downcast eyes. Why was the world so sad, she wondered vaguely? But, like all children must, she bore its misery with patient resignation. If she had had the courage she would have asked someone to take off her liberty bodice with its twenty-two buttons which she had worn since she'd first arrived. It was tight now, and made breathing difficult. Her shoes, too, were small and hurt her feet but she feared that in drawing attention to her increasing size, she might be judged ready for the pot, so she kept silent. In truth, she couldn't really remember how to ask. The word 'I' had completely lost its meaning by now.

Fear and sadness filled her days, punctuated now and then by good things like the sun suddenly coming out and warming her through and through; the taste of warm, newly baked bread from those fearful ovens – the only food she could with any safety eat, knowing for sure she wasn't eating some poor animal or person. Once she had found a little black kitten in one of the barns crying, she was sure, for its mother. They became good friends and she would sneak out in the mornings with her breakfast porridge to feed it and sometimes, if there was any, a cup of milk. She loved the kitten dearly, keeping it all to herself and hugging its memory to her as she climbed the tall stairs to that fearful bedroom, some small defence against the terror of the night.

She was beginning to believe she saw a tiny witch there sometimes, buzzing away in the far corner near the ceiling like a bluebottle, and made sure her eyes never strayed there. Thinking of the kitten helped her keep her eyes tightly shut. No need for nightmares now. Her worst dreams were the ones in which she awoke in her own little bed at home, the sounds of the birds singing in her ears and the sweet milky smell of her mother all around her. The waking was the nightmare and then only the thought of the kitten could stem the flood of her tears.

At times like this she remembered well the past and her great loss and wondered with a fearful passion what it was that she had done wrong to make her parents send her away. She knew she had bitten her sister sometimes and once, at Christmas, having unwrapped the doll her grandparents had given her, thrown doll and wrappings onto the fire. Well it was a boy doll with trousers and everybody knew she hated boys. There was lots of shouting then, but she hadn't cared and had run into the garden and pushed her four-year-old cousin Clive into the goldfish pond as he was a boy too. Oh she wouldn't do things like that now if she could only have another chance: she would be good. So good they wouldn't need to call her Fury any more.

The memories would soon pass, leaving her to get herself through the cold winter days as safely as she could. There was school now in the mornings where it was warm at least. The teacher would say, 'Tut tut. This child is cold and neglected.' Words she didn't understand, but felt must mean there was something bad about her. Oh well. She liked the lady anyway; she had given her a woolly jumper which she loved and wore all the time over her summer frock, even in bed.

School was all right until the day the teacher asked them all to paint her a picture and handed round brushes and paint. The little girl began to shake, covering her ears with her hands and shutting her eyes tightly. When the teacher asked what was the matter she couldn't say; she ran out of the class and up the road. The word painting made her feel afraid and hopeless somehow, she couldn't remember why. She would go and tell the kitten. He always made her smile and might help her to stop shaking.

But the kitten was strange and different that day. She found him in the lane by the cottage, lying down with his eyes open. Probably tired, she thought. She tried to wake him up, waving a stick along the ground in front of him, and tickling him behind the ears as he liked, but it made no difference. Thinking he needed milk, she picked up the limp body and set off for the barn but this time she was spotted by the wolf woman who was pumping water from the well.

'Wot you got there then?' she enquired, waddling over. 'Let me have a look.' The child hung on. No, she would not let her even see it. She knew what happened to animals in this house; had seen the rabbits and chickens hanging upside down with their legs tied. Skinned alive.

She began backing away, about to run, when the woman grabbed hold of her. 'You've killed it, you silly little bitch. That's what you've gone and done,' she exploded, slapping the child about unmercifully, 'and I'll show you what we do to people like you.' Picking the child up by her hair, she flung her into the woodshed and locked the door.

For a while she felt like Brer Rabbit when he had been thrown into the middle of the briar patch, for wasn't that just where she wanted to be? Hidden and safe from everyone, to try and wake her kitten up. 'Wake up please. Wake up and play with me,' she pleaded again and again, tickling and stroking and rocking the cat backwards and forwards in her arms. But it wouldn't and slowly, almost before her horrified gaze, its substance began to change from someone soft and wobbly to something hard and stiff in her hands. She dropped it in horror, walking round and round the shed rubbing her hands together to get the strange feel of the animal off as her panic rose.

The sky was now completely dark, and the shed a black and frightening place of strange shapes and noises. She could scream, but what for?

The witch came then, diving down from the ceiling, laughing and mocking her with, it seemed to the child, the stiff dead body of the cat on its broomstick and all the hobgoblins and foul friends from all the stories and books that she had ever known. She howled then, like an animal, there in the shed crouched up against a woodpile, screaming out for her life and her sanity with no one to hear her but some cruel indifferent children or the big bad wolf.

Everyone noticed she was different after that. Restless, unable to keep still, needing always to be on the move, walking and rubbing her hands together and however hard her teacher tried, she couldn't keep her sitting at her desk for long. She never spoke at all now, and found it difficult to see unless she closed one eye or the other. To keep them both open made everything slide about and blur.

No safe corners now. Everywhere she went was filled with fear. Keep moving. Keep the images away, of half-eaten animals, pigs boiled alive, a sheep too, upside down, its legs stiff in the air, still, not moving. Once she had liked to watch the sheep in the fields, but this one spoiled it. He didn't move, but his tummy got fatter and fatter till one day one of the bad boys poked it with a stick and it exploded, spraying the child with the contents of its rotting guts. Now its memory joined the rest, and the kitten and the witch owned the world, flying freely now in the daytime too, buzzing and swooping wherever she looked. Keep moving. Oh, keep moving.

This is how they found her when the old black car drew up

unexpectedly one spring morning, walking round and round the yard, her shoulders up, her head down, wringing her hands like Lady Macbeth. There was anger then from the two wolf parents. Shouts of 'She's blue with the cold and filthy' and 'We thought you were taking care of her'. Then she and her sister were bundled into the back seat of the car and driven away.

'Why are you smiling, Coral?'

I'm remembering being taken to my grandmother Milson's house, and how she washed me all over with a warm flannel then wrapped me up in a big soft towel.

It was nearly two years later that this little bedraggled Red Riding Hood finally walked out of the pages of her nightmare fairy-story book and into a real grandmother's kitchen, but by then it was too late, she was unable to tell fact from fantasy, distinguish friend from foe, grandmother from wolf.

Everything that moved, that lived, that breathed was a threat to her very existence and the kindness of her grandmother only served to fan the flames of her fears. Was this not just some different kind of game to lure her off her guard, the easier to be caught and eaten? The few things that didn't frighten filled her with a terrible aching sadness, causing her eyes to brim with tears and her grandmother to ask, 'What's the matter, my duck?' with such a worried look on her face that she felt the 'matter' must be that her looks were changing and becoming as terrible to see as she felt herself to be inside. She learnt to hide the tears and when, finally, her parents got a house nearby for them all to live in again she kept well away from them. For might they not send her back to the wolf?

She continued to live in fear of her life, eventually forgetting why. There were so many moves, so many new schools – six before she was seven years old. Her father was a restless, unfulfilled spirit who could never settle in any job for long, a wild outspoken artist unable to say yes when he meant no. He would tell his employers where to stuff their jobs, and so, heigh-ho, up they would go and move, like gypsies, on again. Each new move pushed her further and further into her silent and terrifying world of unsolved mysteries.

Nothing was ever said of her terrible ordeal. A thing called evacuation was often mentioned, but that sounded like the jab that she had once had in her arm, not anything to do with the past.

However, unlike many other children, this little girl was lucky. She had a kind and loving mother who treated her always with tenderness, and a father who understood well how real the fears of children are. Although neither was ever trusted by the child again they never gave up trying to win her confidence. Many a time she would have loved to fling herself into her mother's arms and beg, 'Tell me, please, are you really a wolf?' but that took a courage she didn't possess.

Time passed. She learned to pretend, then one day forgot she was pretending, till thirty years or so later the wolf came back to claim her, as the nightly terrors began. She had no way of knowing then that her happy family life had the whole of the Third Reich stacked up against it; that had she stayed in London she would almost certainly have been killed. The house in Tooting took a direct hit, and her parents had done what they probably believed to be for the best.

Well, now she had a real wolf-tamer on her side, and together they were putting the wolf back where he belonged in time and space; where he could no longer jump out of the shadows unexpectedly, disguised as some other person or thing to disturb her days and haunt her nights.

We smile at each other, the therapist and I. 'Journey's end?' he enquires. Oh no. Not quite. It isn't that easy, for still I find that Little Red Riding Hood's cloak sticks to my shoulders, refusing to be thrown off however hard I try. No, no one else can take it off, it's something I hope to do for myself. But there's the next session, and the next, and the one after that, and all the sessions it may yet take to set me free.

EIGHT

'Let's paint it red.' 'What, the kitchen?' 'No, the whole house. Bright poppy red.' 'You're crazy, Coral. You can't paint everything red. It'll look dreadful.'

'She's red mad. Red car, red boots, red coat – bet she's got red drawers on an' all! Let's have a look!'

Long discussions into the pros and cons of painting the house red went on for days. 'Yeah! Yeah! Yeah!' yelled all the optimists. 'Be careful,' urged the pessimists, 'how about beige?' But red it was, and I thought that with dark brown beams, curtains and carpets it was the loveliest colour I had ever seen.

Deep into my therapy now. Good days and very, very bad ones, grey and fearful: after some sessions I was sometimes so scared I had to curl up in bed for a while with a hot-water bottle and lots of patting and hugging from the children, who understood absolutely, without need for explanation, just how awful the world can seem sometimes.

Well into my training too. A smart-arsed trainee analyst, with patients. 'So whatsya problem, Quasimodo?' Well, not quite that bad. In danger, in fact, of becoming one of the caring, sharing, empathetic, holding crew! Restrain yourself, Coral. These people are also tough survivors, fighting the devil as you are. They need a giant-killer not a good, well-meaning auntie. 'Yes sir, yes sir,' I say to my tutor. 'Tough's the word, but not too tough, eh.' Just listen; see what's going on behind what they say. Why do they say it? Why ask you how you are when they come into room? Is that what they really mean, or are they saying, 'Do you care how I'm feeling?'

Oh it's so difficult when what you really want is a nice chit-chat with them, responding to their sweetness and charm in a like way. But no. Keep your mouth shut. Don't smile, don't nod or shake your head. Don't gasp in amazement at some of the outrageous things you hear. Just keep schtumm and try to look as if you know everything but are prepared to divulge little or nothing of it to them. This is not easy for me, always one for putting people at their ease. Now I had to bear their discomfort and, in fact, make it even more uncomfortable by my lack of spontaneity.

'Can't I even ask her how her mother's operation went?' 'If she wants you to know, she'll tell you.' 'But I want to know!' A therapist has no desires for her patient. Wants nothing more than that they turn up and pay. Sounds so hard and brutal.

'Well can't I just ask . . .?' But of course I learnt that the last thing you can do is just ask. All you get are pat answers.

My very first training case was a clinical psychologist with more qualifications than I'd had nervous breakdowns. 'Oh Lord,' I felt like saying, 'why don't you sit here and I'll lie on the couch!' A man in his middle thirties, endlessly tormented by his inability to be a better person, cure everyone and understand everything. So serious. Not a spark of humour to be seen, and such a brilliant mind.

I sat before him, inwardly quaking but maintaining nonetheless my know-it-all, seen-it-all expression and longing sometimes to drop to one knee and sing 'Mammy' to him, or hang from the light socket and yell one of Martin's brain surgeon hymns. Anything to make him smile. Maybe a Groucho nose and moustache might do the trick! But I swear if I'd worn one he wouldn't even have noticed, just continued his tirade against his poor self.

If he had been a child it would have been easy. I could cuddle or tickle him and tell him I thought he was lovely just the way he was, but no, no – perish the thought! That would have been construed as seductive, so I listened instead.

'Am I boring you?' he asked one day. 'Yes,' I replied, 'and I find myself wondering why, when there must be so many things you want to say that aren't boring.' He cried then. Small teardrops coursed down his stony face. 'Forgive me,' he murmured, 'making a fool of myself.' 'Oh but tears aren't foolish, they're real. They're about things that really hurt, straight from the soul.'

He told me then that the tears were of guilt for the way he had let his father, an eminent psychiatrist, down. Couldn't stay the course. Could only be a psychologist. How hard it was on his poor parents to be saddled with such a failure of a son. They had such high expectations of him and he had failed them. 'Poor you as well, perhaps, to feel so bad,' I said. But this he couldn't concede. He was the bad child: they were never the bad parents. How was I going to get him to see that he wasn't here to fulfil his parents' ambitions, but his own desire and wishes, that his life belonged to no one but himself? *I* couldn't say it; he would have run away, I knew. He was going to have to tell me himself one day. It was going to take a long, long time, but at least we'd begun.

After each session I had to write down what had taken place and present it to my tutor, my supervisor and, once a week, to my peer group. My tutors and supervisors were very kind, on the whole, and seemed to like what I did. My peers, on the other hand, could be savage and intimidating, most of them coming from one or other of the professions – psychiatrists, psychologists, doctors, etc. – with very firm ideas on what was good and what was bad psychotherapy.

'But for God's sake, Coral! Surely you can see when he mentioned how he didn't like his mother's apple dumplings he was talking of the breast! Oedipus, my dear. Pure Oedipus!' Murmurs of 'The breast, the breast. Oh my God! Oedipus! Oedipus!' rang round the room and all became jubilant; ecstatic, I may say. I expected that any minute they would all break into a knees-up or do the hokey-cokey over the chairs and tables. 'You flop the left breast out, you flop the left breast in, you flop the left breast out and you shake it all about . . .'

Well, being well-mannered and very restrained, they instead merely allowed themselves little collusive smiles of smug delight, leaning back into their chairs as if all were privy to some vast secret knowledge that the rest of humanity was just too thick to understand.

One thing they were all agreed upon: therapy was sired by Oedipus, out of Breast. Hallelujah, praise the lord, and pass us a copy of the Collected Works!

'It ain't necessarily so!' I want to scream. 'Fuck Oedipus and the breast.' 'Exactly, Coral. Just what we mean.' Oh hell! 'Where's your sense of humour?' 'You conceal yourself with your humour, Coral.' 'Maybe I reveal myself!' 'You reveal your concealment.'

Oh what the hell. There is absolutely no use arguing with a roomful of trainee therapists. One, maybe two, even three, perhaps, but where four or more are gathered together, it's much better to keep your ideas to yourself and your mouth shut. Some smart-alec will always get the better of you, and, sadly, they will always be plausible and probably right.

But they never won me over, as in all my years of living, laughing, playing, eating, bathing and, yes, sleeping, too, with disturbed children, twenty-four hours a day, seven days a week, fifty-two weeks of the year, I had never once seen Oedipus or the breast get a look in. Vast industries of therapeutic thought seemed to have been founded on the concept of infantile sexuality, children's sexual desires for their parents' bodies, as if it were fact; backed up by the Oedipus legend, which could just as easily be seen as the mother's desire for her son's body. Maybe it's the adults after all who do the desiring; crush and repress it, then lay it at the feet of their children. Perhaps, after all, Freud's patients were right. Maybe their fathers did seduce them and they weren't all hysterical storytellers. And as for the poor man and his apple dumplings, I opted for the fact that he

116

was trying to tell me how defenceless he felt against his mother's femininity, and mine, and hoped I wouldn't be as ruthless with him as she had been. But then I was only a first-year student. We would see!

Life at home was back to normal. It was nearly a year since my stout-hearted Jody had put through a reversed charges call from somewhere in the Midlands, crying and saying why hadn't I written to her? Her social worker had told her that I knew where she was and would contact her if I wanted to see her. She was cold, hungry and sad, she said. Her daddy hit her with his belt and the house didn't even have a lavatory. They had to walk into town each time they wanted to go to the toilet.

Of course, Chris and I fastened on our six-shooters and set off for a show-down at high noon with the social services somewhere up north. We agreed to meet at the girls' home, the only inhabited house in a row earmarked for demolition; windows boarded up, paper peeling off the walls and only two rooms habitable.

'I didn't want to bring them away from you to this,' the mother wept. 'The social workers just kept on at me.' Well, be that as it may. I always take parents with a pinch of salt and never blame them either way. They wouldn't be in need of a social worker if they could handle life on their own. We were all supposed to be there to help them, though as I eyed the father's large studded belt round his jeans, I didn't feel quite so charitable. Wanted to wrap it round his neck and hang him with it, frankly.

The sheriff and his posse arrived on time. Social worker, team-leader and head of department, angry and ready for battle. How dare I interfere? What was I doing there? And would I please leave immediately, the children were no longer my concern. And how dare they, I retaliated, lie to the girls and tell them I knew where they were, implying that I didn't care enough to contact them. They had been in my care for nine years which made them more my business than anyone else's.

Well, so it went on until one of the three, in desperation, turned to the two little sisters huddled in a corner. 'Who do you want to live with? Come on! Speak up! What have you both got to say for yourselves?' – a thing I would never have put them through. It forced them to choose in front of their parents, and to shoulder all the responsibility for that choice, and the guilt it would carry either way. However bad Mother may be, she is a magic person to her children, and it takes a brave, mature one to reject her face to face.

We held our breath. The die was cast and there was no way I could now spare them. Jody took a deep breath and with tears running down her cheeks whispered, 'Coral. I want to live with Coral.' Ann could only hang her head and nod her agreement as I felt her hand slip into mine. Jody edged up closer to Chris. 'Sorry, Mummy,' she murmured, 'I didn't mean to hurt you.'

Oh how much I loved her tender little generous heart. But her mother seemed not to hear, just began talking to the father about the child benefit being stopped. The social workers, after going into a huddle for a while, emerged to state that there were no fees available to place the children back in care with me.

Chris and I looked at each other, smiled, then as he hoisted Jody onto his shoulders I grandly told them to stuff their fees where they kept their one brain cell. The girls were now my guests, welcome to stay as long as they liked, and if one social worker set foot on my land I'd set the dogs on them. Well, the dog. I thought of toothless old Charlie. I'd get more. A pack of Dobermanns if necessary. And leaving them for once speechless, we drove triumphantly home where we were greeted as if we had returned with the Holy Grail.

And so peace reigned for a while. Money, always too tight a problem to mention, was for a moment solved as my dear friend Glenda Jackson, having done a television commercial, sent part of her fees to me. Oil in the boiler, wood in the shed, warm and cosy and happy. Boots on their feet and gloves on their hands, ready to greet the winter properly for the first time since we'd been there.

They were all growing up now, changing; teenagers some of them. Sex was rearing its ugly head, not that I saw it that way. To me, the fact that the girls were giggling over boys and the boys had rude pictures stuffed under their pillows was a cause for celebration as it meant that everything was working the way it should. I read somewhere that the onset of a girl's first period was a feast day for some tribe or other, and I can see why. No, they didn't need to hide their pictures or their passions from me, although in each of us there must be a place where no mother, however much she loves you, may trespass.

So I kept my distance, trying never to belittle first love, knowing how my first love had fashioned my whole life.

'So what's it like then, sex?' asks a curious, thirteen-year-old Harry. 'What does it feel like?' 'Well . . .' I thought it over for a while, 'it's about as good as a Macdonalds and a milk shake when you're starving hungry.' 'That good!' 'Mm. Maybe even a bit better.' 'Cor! Let's try it then!' They all yell and dance round the room. Oh Lord! '*But*, only with someone you love.' That old cop-out! Only if it's with someone you lust after with your whole being, I wanted to say, as I recalled my own glorious nights in white satin, or rough sackcloth – what did it matter if passion ruled the day.

So I wasn't strictly honest with my children. Dark, primeval fears of them all becoming sex maniacs filled my head, though in all honesty I have never come across anyone whom too much sex has harmed (AIDS aside). It's no sex at all that's the killer. But dare you say that to children? Oh foolish me! My children have a modesty and a dignity that transcends all of my feeble teachings. I should have more faith.

'Save yourself for the one you love. Wait! Wait! Be certain he's Mister Right.' So say all mothers, but oh how I wish I had thrown myself away into the arms of my first love. Blond was the colour of my true love's hair; his face was soft and wondrous fair. Brown eyes and high cheekbones; half-Apache Indian. Tall

119

and lithe and wicked and eighteen. And me, small and plain and shy and fourteen. How could we fall in love? But we did.

'Who are you then, kid?' 'Um, I'm Sylvie's sister.' Sylvie, in the middle of the huge dance hall doing the boogie-woogie all over the floor, surrounded by admirers. Me, clutching the sides of my chair, head down, praying that the fat spotty bloke opposite wouldn't ask me to dance again although, to be truthful, he was the only one who had all evening.

I'd worn my best dress, let out my long plaits, and put a pink ribbon round my head to match it, and I thought I looked quite grown-up in Sylvie's high heels. But it was the same every Saturday. Same chair; same lame ducks; same feelings of shame when it was time to go home. A failure. But then how could I hope to compete with my gloriously beautiful red-headed sister, always the centre of every crowd? What had I got to offer compared to her?

'Well, would you like to dance, Sylvie's sister?' I looked up into the face of the young man who had spoken and wanted to die with embarrassment. He was so beautiful it must be some kind of joke he was playing, or maybe he just felt sorry for me. I shook my head and lowered my eyes. I wasn't going to be made a fool of for anybody. 'Hey, you've got brown eyes too! We should stick together.' And as he was about to sit beside me, somebody barged into him, spilling his beer all over me.

Well, there was a glorious punch-up, which I joined in. I can never resist a good fight, and at the end of it we both emerged a bit battered and torn, but firm friends.

So we walked. By the river, through the fields and round the streets of the town, seeing very little except each other. He was in the American Air Force. A troublemaker, they said, reckless and untameable, and I was afraid to tell him my full name or where I lived for fear he would rush over and my parents would put a stop to me seeing him.

A year went by. I was fifteen when I learnt that he was being given a dishonourable discharge and shipped home. He got a message to me through a friend, saying would I give him my address and he would send for me on my sixteenth birthday. So I wrote it all down, sealed it tight with instructions not to open it until he got home, then sat back, my tummy filled with a terrible excitement at my tremendous secret, and I waited.

I waited. And I got to be sixteen and still I waited. Surely tomorrow . . . the next post, or the next. When the phone rings again it will be him – oh please let it be him! I would have left everything I loved and held dear; run away and never looked back. He had only to ask me.

I was at art school now. I liked the other students with their wild rebellious spirits and their burning ambitions to be the greatest, the best, the most original since Van Gogh. Wished I too could care with my whole soul, but half of me was lost somewhere in Georgia.

Finally, when I got to be seventeen I could bear it all no longer. I ran away and married the first man who asked me. Who cares! If I couldn't have my love anyone would do. But did it have to be J.J.?

Many years and many miseries later, some fifteen years or so, I visited the States and looked him up in the Georgia telephone directory. There were five people with his name, an unusual one, so I sent off a postcard to them all and on my return home there was the letter I had been waiting all my life, it seemed, to receive.

He told me how his wallet with my address had been stolen on board ship; how he had written to the mayor of my home town, with nothing but my first name to go on, even contacted the BBC to find me; then, despairing, had married some four years later and now had a little brown-eyed daughter called Coral.

And so I'd got it all wrong; I'd thought I knew all about love and what a sham it was: then learned I knew nothing at all. Too late, of course, but oh! His face was still the one I searched each crowded room to find until one dark day, gazing blindly round a half-empty restaurant in despair, four days after my beloved father had died, I saw the face again. Well no, not quite, the eyes were blue and the accent different, but we seemed to recognise each other instantly, and looked in amazement, wondering where we'd met before.

Is that all there is to it, then? Is it no more difficult than lifting my eyes from the floor? Too easy, far too easy, and so it turned out to be. We spent three days together, then were not to meet again for four years.

NINE

I have never believed in fairies – not since I was very small. Witches, yes; flying around everywhere up to their wicked devious ways. So, when I encountered the good fairy of the west, I found it difficult to recognise her at first. Beautiful, certainly. Tall, willowy and blonde, bursting with American vitality and enthusiasm for all life had to offer.

'Well,' she said, on meeting me, 'I read about you and your children in a magazine in some beauty parlour back in LA and said to myself, I've got to help that lady but, well, one thing and another, I forgot. That was five years ago or so, but then I remembered and, well, here I am. So what do you need? I have only to wave my wand. I'm rich – stinking filthy rich.'

Wow! In fact, wow, wow, wow!! What could this little stammering country bumpkin reply to all that! This just couldn't be for real.

'Oh ha, ha, ha ... you don't have to give me anything, honestly, it's really so kind!'

'Cut the crap. Everybody needs something, and with all these kids you sure as hell do.' Well, you could say that again.

'Perhaps we could do with a little help with our oil bill so that we could keep the central heating on a bit longer in the winter.'

'Oh come on! I'm talking big bucks here.' She strode elegantly through the house in her glorious lynx coat. 'Frankly, Coral,' she said at last, eyeing it all with disapproval, 'this

123

place is a dump and a fucking cold one at that. Let's start there.'

As if by magic, with one wave of her diamond-studded wand, all the draughty old multi-smashed windows were shiny new and double-glazed. Oh this can't be happening to me! Pinch me someone, wake me up.

Next, the kitchen was replaced with a gleaming new white one and on being told the astonishing fact that none of us could ski, she sent us all away for two weeks to learn!

Ay, ay, ay, like the cats that got the cream we smiled and we smiled as we zoomed down the slopes and sipped our après-ski cocktails, this is more like it. This is, in fact, what we deserve and where we belong, we all felt. How could cruel fate have deprived us for so many years of what was rightfully ours? But we all loved the lady too, and would have loved her, I'm sure, had she breezed in with nothing. Loved her for her sweetness, for her passion and the joy she seemed to get from being alive. And when she bought a large house in London to set up a second children's home, our hearts were bursting with gratitude and love. People like her weren't for real, we had always believed. Surely there must be something she wants from us in return.

'What can I give you?' I said again and again. 'What can I possibly offer you in return for all this sweet generosity?' 'Nothing,' she replied. 'Being rich isn't all it's cracked up to be. It's a trap you can't get out of. Imagine walking down a street knowing you can afford everything you see − houses, cars, clothes, you name it. It's scary. A world with no barriers.' Well yes. The therapist in me could dimly see what she meant, but still I felt a fearful sense of imbalance in our relationship. Perhaps being close to the children was enough for her and gave her the framework she felt she needed to feel secure.

So now I began again. The requests to take children in the London house came flooding in. Terrible, terrible cases of cruelty where rape now seemed to be the name of the game. A six-year-old boy raped by his foster father; a little girl of eight sent out whoring round the neighbourhood by her stepfather, not allowed back into the house until she'd earnt £10 each night. Little children on locked wards of mental hospitals, one so filled with despair he'd tried to hang himself at the age of six. All battered and bruised and ripped apart. Where do you begin?

One of the first children I was asked to take believed herself to be in a chamber of horrors where she was tortured each day and would scream and wail as the terrible weapons began their hideous work on her. No, you couldn't see anything, but I knew well how real the pain felt to her. Wrapped in my grandmother's soft bath towel, lying in her big safe bed with the eight-hour nightlight on the wash-stand and a painting of an angel on the wall to watch over me, I was still alone, in hell. When there's nothing tangible left to fear, the real terror begins, as any shell-shocked survivor from any battle front bears witness to.

Some of the acts of cruelty I read about in the case histories would never reach the front pages of newspapers but were to me as grotesque and unbelievable as any exposé on the cover of the *Sun*. A little boy of seven, fostered since he was a baby, believing that these were in fact his real parents and his real home, woke one summer morning to find two suitcases in the hallway. 'Are we going on holiday, Mummy?' he asked. 'No,' replied his mother, 'we are all moving to live by the seaside and we don't want to take you so someone is coming to take you away.' 'But Mummy, don't you love me!' he wept again and again. 'No,' came the reply, 'and I'm not your real mummy anyway. You're only a foster child.' And so a social worker appeared and he was led away where no kind arms were open to receive him, and was passed round and round from foster home to foster home – fourteen in three years.

'This boy finds it difficult to trust and make close relationships.'

'Is untrustworthy and uncommunicative.'

'Shows no affection.'

And so the rejections and excuses for them went on, making

me feel dizzy and ill as I read. 'And this child,' I wanted to add, 'has a broken heart.'

So hard to choose between one child and another, but we only had seven places on offer so decisions had to be made and I opted for the youngest children as I felt we could do more for them. But since I had begun in 1972, the rules had changed drastically, and each child had to be fostered many times before being considered for a placement in a 'caring', therapeutic, ongoing, long-term, one-to-one small family unit, as I discovered to my alarm my homes were now called.

So it was seldom possible to get my hands on any child under ten with less than twelve or so changes of foster folk. One girl I heard of had had twenty-two in two years and was, not surprisingly, over whatever hill it was that sanity teetered on the brow of.

I took one fourteen-year-old toughie whose first words to me were, 'You'll never break my spirit, you fucking old cow,' after which he threw the stereo system which we had bought to delight him through the closed window. Heigh-ho! Here we go again! Had to admire him, though, and could quite understand his reluctance to believe that anyone wanted to do anything but tame the tiger in him, not shine up its coat and sharpen up its claws.

This boy had come from the secure unit of a detention centre where he had been talked sensibly to by a series of child psychologists, educational psychologists, clinical psychologists, probation officers and social workers daily. 'We only want what's best for you, and what's best for you is to do what we want,' seemed to be the message that got across, as relayed to me by him.

'Well,' I said, after hearing all this, 'I'm quite different. I don't want what's best for you. I want what's best for me, because you're right – I am a fucking old cow!' We eyed each other up, him not quite sure if I was for real. 'At least you're a fucking honest one,' he said at last, after which we both laughed and a little of the tension was taken out of our first meeting.

The house shook for a while as Hoe Benham had done before it. Everything was smashed up almost before it had been bought. Foul language and rude gestures through the windows had the neighbours up in arms, and pretty soon we were surrounded by barbed wire, a bit like Colditz.

'They were miming masturbation at me in the garden!' cried a frail, very genteel old lady. You bad, bad boys! You'll all go blind! 'Up yours, Atkins.' Well, okay, if you say so.

It takes time. First of all they have to show you how bad they are. They'll get better, I pleaded with the local citizens. 'Please. Give us a little while. A year from now you won't know it's a children's home at all.' So, amazingly, they agreed, and at the end of the first year, Hilary, a wonderful young woman I had met some years before through therapy, who ran the home for me, Marion, Steve and the rest of the team, had a happy, peaceful (well fairly!) bunch of children on their hands who were learning to take out their anger and frustration at the world inside their home and with the people who took care of them, leaving the neighbours to continue their peaceful existence.

But they were very very ill, most of them, with such a fragile hold on reality. The ten little ones I had started off with in the first house had all been under six; unlike them, these children had many years of anger, rage, terror and rejection to cope with. So many, often I feared that getting them better was an impossible task. At least with little children you can pick them up if all else fails, but with a twelve-year-old boy, bigger and tougher than you are in every way, it just wasn't a possible option.

Tender loving care was still top of my list; patting, hugging and looking for the damaged little three-year-old behind all the adolescent aggression. No, not words really. Just constantly proving by our actions that we wouldn't reject them, whatever they did. Neither would we be seduced by their adult cunning into giving in to them endlessly for the sake of peace. Firm, strong boundaries inside which anything was possible and everything forgivable.

Although I kept a close eye on the new home, I had always known that I could only be a kind auntie to the children there. There just wasn't enough of me to go around. To be any use to a damaged child, it is essential to become the centre of their lives, drawing both their hatred and their love in like measure, a task I had to entrust to the people who ran it. I now had fourteen children at Hoe Benham to take care of, as well as my own dear son Harry, with whom I felt I wanted to spend more and more time alone to give us both a chance to live a normal family life together before he grew up and I lost him forever. He was busy on his O-levels now, had already sailed through two a year early, and I was a very proud mum.

We took a house in London, which I also used as a consulting room for my psychotherapy practice, and I began to learn what a lovely son I had and how lucky I was. He had given me such an easy ride: one I didn't deserve. I always seemed to be busy patching up other people's problems, taking him completely for granted. Harry, pay me back one day. Let me have it right between the eyes. Never, in the whole of his time at Hoe Benham, had he used me against the children, been jealous or vindictive against these people he was forced to share his mother with. He fought all his own battles, never pulled rank and was full of the devil too. I was certainly one of the undeserving and I knew it, trying to make it all up to him at once.

'Pack it in, Atkins,' he would say laughingly, 'you're trying too hard. You'll never get it right.' Well, I shall keep trying until I do. No get-out clauses for me, no mitigating circumstances. Once you have a child it must come first, the only absolute I knew, and I had failed to see the wood for the trees. So suffer, Miss Atkins, you stand accused, despite the fact that your son has a dynamic all his own enabling him to soar above all your shortcomings.

Peter did his best to be a good daddy, but it was at times a poor best. He was now a falconer to some Saudi Arabian prince, had a whole valley in a mountain range cordoned off there, and bred birds of prey, which of course meant he was seldom in England. It was fun for Harry, who sometimes accompanied him up hill and down dale in search of rare species for the breeding centre, no cliff-face too steep for the pair of them, like mountain goats. I joined them once in Morocco, watching with my heart in my mouth as my two heroes scaled some giddy height. We had planned the trip as a possible reunion to see if perhaps we could be a family once again but, oh, when Peter caught a wild falcon, put a bag over its head and tied it to a post, I wept, and pleaded with him to let it go, which of course only hardened his resolve not to, telling me it would be better off in his valley, fed and cared for.

Poor old Harry, piggy-in-the-middle of all this. I even offered to buy the falcon off Pete, but to no avail. So I left in a huff a few days early, to drive his minibus which he said I could have if I could get it home to England.

I set off full of righteous indignation and all went well till, sitting in the docks at Tangiers listening to 'Dixit Dominus' and feeling full of goodwill towards all men, except Peter White-head, the two policemen who were going through the formalities of searching my vehicle suddenly became very excited, shouting and jumping about and blowing whistles all over the place, with others running from all directions. Nothing to do with me, I thought, peacefully, I've got nothing to hide. Until one of them held up two telescopic rifles before me which they'd found under the floorboards.

'I should switch off the divine Mr Handel if I were you, young woman,' he said to me, 'you're under arrest.' Well thank you and goodnight! Another fine mess you've got me into, White-head! 'But they're not mine! The van's not mine! Look at the log book!' Couldn't find it, hadn't got one. 'Well look at the insurance documents.' Hadn't got them either. 'Well, my pass-port. Go and speak to Peter: he's living in Marrakesh in the Medina somewhere.' They fell about laughing at this. About five million other people also lived in the Medina. 'Oh God, you must believe me.'

No, they were totally unimpressed with me and all my entreaties, handcuffed me and led me off to jail where, while I sat thinking of *Midnight Express* and never seeing my babies again, the chief of police told me pleasantly with a smile that these were the self-same type of rifle that had shot and killed President Kennedy. 'Oh come on, they're children's air rifles,' I joked, which was true, but it was no laughing matter. Guns of any sort were forbidden in Morocco and I was in dead trouble.

They hung on to me for two days, shouting and bullying and demanding to know where I had hidden the bullets; they strip-searched me and wouldn't even let me go to the lavatory unaccompanied – the worst indignity of all, as the toilets were the sort with a big hole and two large concrete pads for your feet. The guard propped the door open and stood picking his teeth with a match as he watched me cope with all my English modesty till, throwing caution to the wind, nature took over. The relief of Mafeking!

I had to do some serious thinking. How did people get out of this kind of situation? There was only one way I knew. So, getting the chief alone, I began talking about compensating him for all his troubles. What a hard job his was, and how little, I was sure, he got for all his pains.

He looked vaguely interested, so I got out my wallet. One hundred pounds, two hundred pounds. He smiled, but continued playing with the paper clips on his desk, so I fished a bit deeper. Two hundred and eighty-seven was all I could find. His smile broadened. A deal.

I was escorted by him to the van, given my guns, and put on board a ship for Spain where, as the boat pulled away from the dock, I couldn't resist the urge to point the gun at him and pretend to pull the trigger. He was okay, and he laughed, holding up his hands in mock arrest, and I wanted to rush round the boat hugging and kissing everybody. I couldn't believe I'd got away with it, although of course I'd no money to get home, but a few hitchhikers to pay the petrol soon solved that problem.

On finally arriving safe and sound at Hoe Benham once again, the van gave a sigh and collapsed, never to go anywhere else again. What a wasted journey. But I did receive a postcard from Algeria, which simply said, 'I let the bird go in the desert, you witch! Peter.'

No, we were just not cut out to be together, and pretty soon afterwards he married Dido Goldsmith, who put a gossamer bag over his head, tied him with a silken thread by the leg to her family tree and presented him with four beautiful daughters one after the other. You'll never be let loose in the desert again, my friend, but I don't believe you want to be any more.

Goodbye to Harry's days of being spoilt by his father's girlfriends: dined at Trader Vic's by a desperately-in-love Bianca Jagger, jetted across the channel to be cosseted by a tearful Natalie Delon or presented with a portfolio of paintings by a resigned but ever-hopeful Nicky de St Phalle. Just a bunch of sisters to cope with instead.

By the waters of Babylon – well the Thames, actually – we sat down and wept, Harry and me, the day we heard he was to be married. Why, I can't say. Perhaps because he wasn't to be ours exclusively any more.

TEN

We were right to weep, things were never the same again. But on the whole not too bad either, and I couldn't grumble, there was usually some man or other in my life who reckoned he loved me. Trouble was, like Goldilocks and the bowl of porridge, they either blew too hot or too cold, too crazy and manic, or too deadly dull and safe, wanting either to bash me up or take care of me endlessly, and of course any weaknesses they had were impossible to hide from the children. 'What do you think of him then, kids?' I would ask eagerly as I fell in love yet again. 'Isn't he *lovely*!' Pause. 'Um . . . yes . . . but well, oh nothing.'

'No, no, no! Be honest. Be brutal!'

'Well, he's nice . . . but his legs aren't very long are they? And is one of them wooden? Only he seems to limp a bit, and he squints.' Harry was more straightforward. 'Urr! *Coral*! Not him, are you mad? He looks like a sponge pudding on legs.' Love found it hard to survive such scrutiny, and they were always right.

I did find a nice actor-writer, whom I was very fond of. He wrote plays about me, and lovely songs for me, and played cricket with Harry. And he could have been almost right, but I have a cold and ruthless heart, which I find hard to give away. It's never satisfied, always believing that just round the corner lies perfection. Hold out, heart, who knows?

I was learning so much about myself through my work with

132

the guild. I had a full quota of patients now, and was beginning to learn how to learn to be a good therapist. Seems to me you can only be taught what *doesn't* work; what *does* work is down to you, and whatever unique qualities you may or may not have within you to speak directly to someone's fears and joys, bypassing the ego altogether, which leads us up so many cul-de-sacs.

Working in such close proximity with all kinds and classes of people, I found they all had one thing in common: when they were honest and straightforward and themselves, they were all beautiful, dignified and godlike, each one seeming to possess a little bit of pure gold within them, underneath all the anger, fear and confusion. Each one striving in their own way to give and receive justice.

At least the children I had taken on since I opened Hoe Benham were beginning to stand up and be counted; their wolves and demons were at last laid to rest. Two had six O-levels apiece and were going on to do their As. And the one who had been bullied so, ended up as a super-hero, head boy of the school, captain of the soccer and athletics team, and someone whom nobody pushed around any more.

Jody sailed through secretarial college with flying colours, and all of them in their own way were slowly getting what they wanted for themselves from life. The new children were coming along well too.

Sexual abuse was a new venture for me. Did you treat abused children differently from the other kids? I'd heard a lot of talk on the subject, read books, and seen self-conscious doctors and nurses playing with Mummy and Daddy dollies with equally self-conscious and, to my mind, totally baffled children. I began to realise that no, they needed what everybody else in the world needs: one safe person to cling to, one safe place to be. When they really are safe, the words will come tumbling out, and not a moment before.

How I wondered about all the little children who phone Childline. Is there really anybody there for them? Or will they, like lots of my children before they came to me, be thrown out of the frying pan and into the fire?

In many of the cases I came across, sex was the least of the children's problems. What was really disturbing was the sadism that accompanied it, the cruelty and lack of love. One little girl cried to go back to the man who had abused her since she was four. It was better than being with a foster mother who beat her and sent her to bed without supper because she'd been sick on the hall carpet. 'At least he wasn't cruel to me,' she wept, 'at least he gave me my dinner.'

I never failed to be amazed at the sweetness of my children. At one point it was necessary to take a little girl of eleven to court to face her seducers: four men who thought gang bangs with children a pleasant way to spend the evening after the pubs closed.

We duly arrived at the courthouse, and there they sat in smart suits with shirts and ties to match, all trying to look like four of the holy apostles who had wandered in there by mistake. 'Who me, sir? What sir, no sir, never sir, she's lying sir, making it up your honour.'

They were all pleading innocent, forcing the poor little girl to give evidence. I had to leave her for a couple of minutes to speak to the court officials. On returning I found her in tears: all too much, obviously, I thought.

But no, the tears weren't for her at all. One of the men had brought his sixteen-year-old girlfriend and their three-month-old baby and it was for the baby that the tears were shed.

She was lying in her carry-cot, blue with cold, wearing only a summer dress and a nappie. It was eight degrees below zero outside. My little girl took me to one side. 'We must do something for the baby, Coral,' she wept. 'I've got some pocket money here, and if you'll lend me a bit more I'll go and buy her some warm clothes.'

So off she went, returning with half of Mothercare, and when the child's father saw what was going on, he burst into tears too, changing his plea to guilty. So at least in this case justice was seen to be done. Due only, of course, to the child's tender heart.

Was there a pattern to the sudden surge in cases of child abuse? The only common denominator I could find myself was that many of the children concerned had been left in the care of stepfathers. Their mothers had taken off with some new man, often a new baby too, and left them, not with the real father, who was usually the man before last, but the current boyfriend.

My friends in social services told me that in cases like that the children would normally have been taken into care, but because of the drastic cuts in spending on child care, and the closure of nine-tenths of all children's homes in the country, there was nowhere to put them, except in equally dodgy and untried foster placements. All the decent foster parents had long ago taken on their quota of kids for the duration of their childhoods.

They were being pressed, they told me, to follow a line of community care, which in their cynical and overworked eyes simply meant no money to spend on this child, leave it where it is and hope that the neighbours will hear and do something. One even told me in desperation that every time a child is battered to death it's one less burden for the state to carry, and a necessary evil in such lean times.

These were personal views, and of course the people involved were powerless to change the system. Also, they relied upon it for their livelihood, and it would have taken a brave, foolhardy one to speak out, stand up and be counted.

The country suddenly seemed to me to be alive with experts on child abuse. There were endless discussions on television with learned men and women with long grave faces lined with deep concern, who had finally found something to be outraged about. A common enemy, at last: the child abuser, making the rest of us feel safe and secure in our virtuous condemnation of such behaviour.

What of all the everyday acts of cruelty that children were expected to bear, once placed in society's loving hands. Who was going to feel outraged about those?

* * *

We had twenty-two children now, under two safe roofs; at least their days in the wilderness were over. How safe were the roofs? Oh very, very, very! I had at last managed to purchase the house at Hoe Benham, due largely to a good deal of help from the owners, and with a fairy godmother to watch over the London one, what could possibly go wrong? Something did, of course. One would have hoped that, after qualifying as an analytical psychotherapist with many years of personal therapy under my belt, and having succesfully run my own children's home for fourteen long hard years, I would have acquired some wisdom and common sense and the ability to discern and discriminate among people and events around me – 'to read it like a book', as they say. Sadly, it would appear that I was still no wiser than on the day I had begun and, due to my extreme naivety, we found ourselves having to leave the London house. There was nothing I could do to salvage the situation; no court of appeal; endless self-recrimination didn't solve anything. We were out and that was that. How could I have been so stupid? How could I have given my word to so many people – social workers, parents, the officials of the DHSS – that we were safe and secure there for ever? What was I thinking about? Oh I was afraid, my stomach in knots, as I watched the little children in the London house taking life a bit more for granted each day, leaning into the house and its very foundations, it almost seemed, and taking their strength from it. Kick them all out? To where for God's sake? *To where*?! Hoe Benham was bursting at the seams; not a square inch for anyone else. The rooms there were already partitioned and repartitioned again to give everybody their little bit of private space.

Buy a place? With what? Rent one? What a joke! Even if we could find somewhere, nobody would take seven seriously disturbed kids. The situation had been taken out of my hands. What could I possibly do?

Should I fall on my knees and pray to a God I didn't have too much faith in anyway and whom I had, in any case, greatly maligned over the years, ranting and raving at him and calling him a silly old fart for making such a cock-up of things? Fancy sending His son down to sort out all the mess. Why didn't He come himself? Oh forgive me, forgive me. Let bygones be bygones. Anything you want, Your Honour, my first edition Nietzsche, or my Gustav Klimt print, if just this once you'll deliver the goods. *Do* something for Christ's sake! Oops, sorry, but you know what I mean.

Now, who says there's nobody out there listening? Even cynical old know-it-all, seen-it-all, me was shaken to the core by the next turn of events.

ELEVEN

Some months before this crisis I had done a broadcast for Gloria Hunniford, expounding my views on child care, and saying that I believed if you took children on then you took them on forever; there were no get-out clauses, and you shouldn't reject them . . . on and on, whine whine whine. I then forgot all about it. But yes! Somebody was listening out there, with ears atune to all I said, nodding in agreement.

A letter arrived. I was afraid by now to open letters, so many threatening ones had I received. There had even been one delivered by hand, simply addressed to the occupiers, which was opened by one of the children who thought it was a circular. To his horror, he read that the house was now on the market and we had one month to leave. Imagine the panic! But today's letter bore a postmark I had not heard of before: Painswick.

'Oh nice, yes, yes, you do, you feel the same? You've had similar experiences? What, personally and professionally? Oh! I see and a cheque for my work. Gosh! Thanks!' And would I like to go to lunch the following Sunday. Yours, Fred.

'P.S. There's a house here I want to show you.'

Very enigmatic, didn't know quite what to make of it, or where Painswick was, and really I'm not a great socialiser, always uneasy with strangers. Still, a kind letter and gesture and I certainly felt I could use all the friends I could get at such a grim time in our lives. So off I dutifully set, on a cold spring morning, thinking of all the things I ought to be doing, and all the worries I ought to be worrying about. But as I got deeper and deeper into the county of Gloucestershire, I simply couldn't help noticing it: gentle, it seemed, though full of wild contrast, deep black valleys and high, soft, downy green hills.

There would be a sudden little town dominated by a number of forsaken Victorian factories following the bed of some small, clear, swift-flowing stream. Everything was built of dignified grey stone.

Painswick itself is to me the village we all seek when we drive into the country on a Sunday afternoon, complete with cafés selling cream teas. Ninety-nine yew trees stand to attention in the churchyard, their leaves clipped to a neat, short-back-and-sides, not a leaf out of place, seeming to whisper together of all things decent, of playing the game. 'And that's not cricket, is it chaps? What!'

Fred was a dear and put me at my ease at once. Just recently retired, he was eager to tell me of his involvement with a charity called Gyde Trust and the work that they had done over the years for children.

It seemed he and his colleagues were also appalled at all the foster breakdowns they had come across, and had even begun to do a nationwide survey to assess just how bad the problem was. It was music to my ears, as sometimes I feel I'm a bit hard on the old foster mothers. But as I only come in contact with the ones who've failed it's difficult to know where all the good ones are.

He and his Trust were very taken by the fact that in my sixteen years of running a children's home I'd never given up on a child or rejected one, and actually had most of my original ones still with me.

'Just how kids in care should be treated,' he said with real passion, having been brought up in care himself.

No mention yet of a house. Maybe it was this one, his own, he wanted to show me. It certainly was beautiful, perched on the edge of the village overlooking a valley with a small lake just visible in the distance. I said as much.

'What, this house? Yes, yes, it is nice. That reminds me, Coral, we had better get up to Gyde.'

Not really knowing what he meant, and not quite wanting to ask, I meekly followed his car back through the village, past the ninety-nine decent chaps, 'Attention! Smarten up, smarten up, yes sir', and on to the Gloucester road where we turned in through some grand gates and into a long and beautifully kept drive, with neatly mown lawns stretching as far as the eye could see, under an arch, and stopped in a courtyard of the most massive and beautiful house I have truly ever visited.

Probably come to pick up the key to the one he wants to show me, I thought cynically; but no.

'Here we are, Coral,' he said cheerfully. 'This is the house I wanted to show you.'

Well, where do you begin? We opened up the huge oak doors and after a few twists and turns I was utterly and hopelessly lost. It was enormous, room after room after room, one going off from another at all angles, the windows all latticed and gabled, the stairs all huge and oak, and so many bathrooms I lost count.

And when we got upstairs I felt quite nervous, and kept close to Fred, feeling I would never find my way out if I lost him.

'About forty in all,' he said cheerfully, 'bedrooms that is. And maybe sixty rooms all told, not counting the three flats and the two cottages, plus of course the school house.'

By now my head was spinning as I opened one door after another, wondering why on earth he wanted me to see it all, apart from its obvious beauty underneath all the garish wallpaper and wildly mismatching furniture and carpets. I soon found out as we finally, oh joy, arrived back where we began. He smiled.

'So, if you want it, it's yours.'

The words took a while to sink in. I'm a bit deaf in any case,

Peter having thumped me once after I had blacked his eye (self-defence on his part). But when they did filter through to the appropriate bits of me, I heard myself saying, 'No, it's very kind but I couldn't even find my way around let alone take it on.'

He laughed again. 'Well, think it over. It's not really all that big you know. Actually I was brought up here.'

I looked back through the door at a huge painting of a grave Victorian gentleman seated in a vast armchair.

'He's the one who built it,' said Fred. 'Old Mr Gyde, he built it specially for kids like yours.'

I looked at the picture again; did I see it wink at me? Oh no, not cracking up again. I escaped off home as soon as I could. Not that I didn't appreciate Fred's company, or his magnificent offer, but I felt a bit like a fieldmouse being offered one of those bigger and better barns, out of my class, just not even worth thinking about. But think of course I did, and eventually took Chris and the kids down there one Saturday just to have a look at what a kind offer we had been made.

'But kids, see what I mean? We couldn't possibly live here, it's much too big.'

I have said many times that my children never fail to amaze me. This day was no exception. To a child they pounced on me, snatching me by the throat and screaming, 'You turned it down? You actually turned this house down? You said no? Are you mad? We love it, I want that room, and I want that one, with its own bathroom, and I bags the snooker table first, all right then I get first go on the tennis court. Oh and can we put the football nets up now and use that hill up there for dirt tracking? Oh yes and how about holding discos on Saturday nights in the school room? We could charge a fiver at the door.'

On and on they went, Chris raising his eyebrows and simply saying, 'They're right, and think, Coral, we could get the London lot in here as well, all safe and sound under one roof.'

It was a sobering thought. I was finding it hard to accept that we would have to move from the London house. 'But the children there are so little and fragile, and this house here so big

141

and frightening. Then there are the friends they have made in London and the schools they feel safe in. Here would be too, oh, somehow too vast for them,' I pleaded.

'Let's ask them,' Chris replied. 'Get them down and just see what happens.'

They reacted in much the same way as my own children had, running and romping and playing hide-and-seek all over the house, wanting everything they saw at first. This, I knew, was a usual reaction of deprived and insecure kids, always believing that a new place, thing or person would be the answer to everything that was bad and frightening. So it was with mixed feelings that I watched them gradually getting closer and closer to Hilary and Steve, hanging on to their arms and hands, knowing perhaps that there lay their real security, and finally asking, 'Can we go home now to London?' A triumph for all the loving and hard work that the staff had put in, but not really helping me solve my dilemma at all. I took my problem to the board of directors, weighing up the pros and cons of staying in London and taking my chances, or retreating to Painswick and at least being sure of a roof over our heads. Another problem for me was time. The Gyde Trust needed an answer within a month as they didn't want to leave the house empty, and another charity, second on their list, was pressing hard.

It was really yes or no, there and then.

My dear Stefan was the first director round the board table to break the silence that had followed the news of our dilemma.

'Take it, Coral,' he said. 'Be brave and do it. We hoped for a miracle when we knew we had to leave the London house; well, this is it.'

Gradually the grave and kindly heads all nodded their agreement. We must move and move fast or we would lose it. It was now March, and the Trust wanted us in by May.

Oh my God. I thought of the sixty glorious rooms to decorate, carpet and furnish, and I aged ten years, not least of my problems being the money to do so. Admittedly, the place already had some furniture and carpets in it, but it was the kind found in most institutions, someone else's cast-off rubbish and just not on; iron beds and couches with the stuffing coming out. No, I could salvage little of it, and would have to start from scratch.

My children must have the very best that I could manage. I owed them that at least. Especially the little ones whom I was uprooting like plants that had only recently been sown, and re-planting in foreign and untried soil.

I agonised over it for days. 'I can't do it to them, it isn't fair,' I told my directors, who, being less passionate and more level-headed, eventually convinced me that the children would have a more secure future at Gyde House. And so I had no choice: I must pack them all up in cotton wool and off we must go.

I was lucky in as much as my sister Sylvia was an interior designer, and on her first sighting of Gyde House her heart leapt for joy. 'Oh, I know exactly what to do with this,' she said enthusiastically. 'It's wonderful. This main corridor' – a hundred yards long may I say – 'we'll do in a warm, dusky apricot.'

It was lime green at the time. My father would have loved it.

'Then a soft, gingery carpet to match, with huge ginger chinese lanterns instead of lamp shades, hanging low, and a lovely Laura Ashley print for the curtains. And then this sitting room here: let's think – dark pink and grey.'

And off she charged followed by my children.

'Er, and how about red for this room?' I was heard to say from time to time, only to have a little hand clapped over my mouth, and 'No reds' yelled in my ears. 'We're sick of reds.' Oh, suit yourselves, at least my consulting room's staying red, let the patients all suffer, I thought spitefully, unable for once to get my own way.

By now we had a month to the deadline on which we were expected to move in and not a dab of paint put on so far. I got hold of my window cleaner in London, who's a very good painter as long as he doesn't get depressed, and a couple of mates of mine, and together with some of the older children we all set to, sloshing on the apricots and pinks and greys with gay abandon, and all taking turns to keep the window cleaner as happy and high-spirited as was humanly possible: no mean task with a depressive like him.

Oh but surely we don't need more paint? Gallons, vats, veritable water towers full of the stuff, and so expensive. And a hundred yards of ginger carpet – you're joking, that much? It can't cost that much, you must have made a mistake. Sadly, pocket calculators never make mistakes.

So with fingers crossed and a very insecure prayer for another move in another mysterious way, 'financial please, your wonderfulness, if possible this time', I continued signing cheques till my arm nearly dropped off.

'Give no thought for tomorrow what ye shall eat or what ye shall wear.' I hope you're right, mate, or we are all going to be a very hungry bunch of flashers!

We were not, of course, able to get it all finished in the month allotted to us, but by the end of June the house was beginning to come together into a warm and welcoming home, which I felt any one of my children would feel proud to live in.

Hilary had done her best to make the London children's section as much like the home they were leaving as possible. She had brought them all down on numerous occasions and was gradually getting them used to the idea of moving, which was no mean feat. My own children couldn't be kept away.

I had divided the whole place into three sections, one for the London kids, one for my own new wild tearaways and a separate ten bedroomed apartment with six bathrooms, no less, for my teenagers, so they could be quite apart from all the violence and tantrums, but still part of the family. (I should explain that most of my original ten children, now in their late teens and officially out of my care, are still and forever part of my family, and have a home with me, while I have one, for as long as I live.)

And so in August, after the annual holiday to Spain, taking a deep breath, touching wood and turning round three times with thirteen black cats sitting on my head for luck, I moved all twenty-five of them in.

Happy ever afterwards, peace in our time, sweetness and reason and light? No chance, forget it. I lost count of the windows that were broken in that first week, the locks wrenched off, the rooms smashed in anger and little boys trying to run home to London. One even made it; we had to leave someone there all the time to catch him and bring him back. Sadly he couldn't adjust; it was one too many moves for him, and he was finally locked away again for his own safety.

I should have expected it, I suppose, knowing how any kind of change can frighten the past alive in them again and provoke the kind of behaviour which brought them to my door in the first place. We tried not to be too cross, but soon the local policeman was making regular appearances, as dark and dastardly deeds were being perpetrated in the small, peaceful village. They weren't all my children's doing, I'm happy to say, but we needed eyes in the backs of our heads to be sure we knew where all the troublemakers were at all times of the day and night.

'Who me? It wasn't me. I was in the billiard room with him.'

'Yeh, that's right!'

'Oh you pair of villains. And put those fags out, you're only twelve, and who climbed up the drainpipe and stood on the roof singing rude songs, I wonder?'

Same old innocent faces, angels sent to delight me from paradise, and it's always as much as I can do not to laugh in situations like this, having great respect somewhere inside me for that devil in each one of them. For two pins I'd like to join them on the roof for a knees-up.

Chris, as usual, in his own calm, joyful and powerful way pulled the whole thing slowly together, calming the ones that needed calming, putting pressure when needed on the wild bunch, and never ever failing to make them all, staff and kids alike, feel loved and valued. If I was handing out halos his is the head one would be placed on for sure.

145

Of the ten children I first began with in 1972, all were winners in one way or another. Several of them had obtained O- and A-Levels, one going on to art college, another to university. One of the girls had become an office manager and one was about to embark on the long, hard slog to become a lawyer. Some were now married with homes and families of their own, and one of the boys was working part-time modelling as the hero of many a photo-romance. The charmer who called me a fucking old cow three short years ago was now at acting school, passionately involved in *Hamlet* and *King Lear*.

As for my best beloved Harry, having finished his exams he took off to work his way round the world and see what it had to offer him, attacking life with a joyful fury and sending me on occasion the most amazing poems, taking my breath away. Harry Whitehead, did he write that? Oh, so proud of you, too, my old trooper who stood tall by my side through it all. And if it's true what they say and there are only hammers and nails in this life it seems I've brought up a family of hammers. No one is ever going to nail any of their feet to the floor again, and I'm proud of them for that. I'm proud of myself too, perhaps.

And so, with a large cheque arriving to help us with the move, they all lived happily ever afterwards in their five-star wonderland in the middle of the glorious Cotswolds, with saints and martyrs like Barbara, Chrissy, Steve and the rest to pander to their every whim.

But as the sun slowly sinks in the west and the Hollywood angelic choirs rise to a crescendo, what about me then God? Where's the pay-off for me for all these deeds of self flagellation?

Dear Mr Atlas, have finished the course, please send the Muscles.

How about me riding off into the sunset, in the arms of some true love? I know, I know, I asked for someone to love me, you gave me no one so that I could love all men. Not good enough, old fruit.

He has a sense of humour, God, I must admit that, or

146

whoever does the shuffling and dealing out of the cards in heaven has.

I fell in love all right, on a cold day in January in 1976 in a café in Austria where my sister and I had gone to mourn the loss of our dear father, in private away from the kids. Suddenly I was looking up into the face I was to love from then onwards, had perhaps loved since I was fourteen. But couldn't it have been the face of some distinguished, slightly greying actor, writer, director or eminent psychiatrist? Or a big shot wheeler-dealer business man, rich beyond imagining? Did it have to be with a penniless German medical student in his early twenties? I was thirty-eight at the time.

Ah, cruel fate. I rushed off home, declaring we must never meet again. I meant it, too, throwing myself with gay abandon into the arms of many new men to try and forget him.

Till one day, four years later, on a wet October evening in 1980, during a break between patients, the door bell rings and there he stands, leaning his lanky six-foot-two frame against the doorpost.

We look at each other for some long time in silence, till smiling he says, 'Well, Atkins, I'm now four years older so what's the big deal?'

Speechless, I could only stammer, 'I have another patient in five minutes.'

'Well, we'd better get a move on then,' he replied, shutting the door behind him. 'We've got a lot of catching up to do.'

He was wild and honest and free, and why I loved him so is hard to tell. Perhaps he brought to mind my first experience of an unbound spirit who saw something I failed to see in me. I was nine at the time, and my parents had taken us on holiday to some seaside town where I found an injured seagull on the beach. Although fearful of its size and wildness, I took it home and tended its battered wings till they could fly again. It was a sad day for me, though, the day my friend took to the skies once more, flapping his huge wings and vanishing without a second glance. The way of the world as I knew it, I thought;

but it seemed I didn't know everything. The next day as I sat on the roof of our beach hut, down he swooped, landing on my shoulder and rubbing his sharp beak and shiny head against my cheek. I knew from that day on that the only kind of love that would be any use for me was the love I'd been given from him, who, having the whole of the vast, limitless sky to fly in had freely chosen to fly back to me.

We were happy, my lover and I. The children loved him too. But we never made any kind of plans for a life together, always believing we should find someone more suitable, closer to our own age and profession, trying and failing and ending up together, again and again, for nine long and joyful years. Expecting nothing from one another, we found we'd got so much; but, as so often with true love, doomed was the word for ours. One day I made him fly away forever.

Marriage? I don't think so; to me getting married is no different from losing your virginity, something which can only happen once with any real credibility. How many times can you promise eternity? He was too much of a lionheart to live in the shadow of what laurels I had gathered in my life, had to go out and earn his own. I hope he makes it, but the world seems afraid of the free, wanting to cage them, and have them all worrying about paying the mortgage on their gilded cages, and quite forgetting their planned flights to Mars or Venus and back before morning. I wasn't going to be the one to put him in my cage.

Ah but it hurts, it hurts – though a little less every day. And with so much love surrounding me from the children, my four dogs, my dear sister Sylvie and her daughter Katie and of course my mother, now eighty-five and still treating me as if I were a baby, and all the good friends who have helped and supported me through the years, dragging me from one crisis to another, I can't claim to be lonely or lost any more. And with no shadows now to disturb my nights, my own wolf tamed at last and walking to heel, when I wake sweating and afraid in the dead, cold hours of the early morning, it's for all the other little children, still lost and alone, wandering in my dark forest.

Oh grandmother, grandmother, who will save the children from the big, bad wolf?

'Happiness; how little attains happiness!'
Thus I spoke once and thought myself wise.
But it was blasphemy: I have learned that now.
Wise fools speak better.
Precisely the least thing, the gentlest, the
rustling of a lizard, a breath, a moment, a
twinkling of the eye – little makes up the quality
of the best happiness. Soft!
The world is perfect.

Friedrich Nietzsche
Thus Spake Zarathustra